BATMAN HAUNTED GOTHAM

Doug Moench
Writer

Kelley Jones
Penciller

John Beatty (Parts 1-3)
Jason Moore (Part 4)
Inkers

Willie Schubert
Letterer

Daniel Vozzo
Colorist

Jones, Beatty & Vozzo
Original Series Covers

BATMAN created by BOB KANE

Cover by Kelley Jones, John Beatty & Daniel Vozzo.

BATMAN: HAUNTED GOTHAM

DC Comics, 1700 Broadway, New York, NY 10019
A Warner Bros. Entertainment Company
Printed in Canada. First Printing.
ISBN: 978-1-4012-2141-6

Hell's Hunting Ground

Haunted Gotham — Part One

BRUCE? YOUR MOTHER THOUGHT YOU MIGHT WISH TO GO OUT WITH US TONIGHT... PERHAPS TO THE THEATER.
Beware all who enter haunted Gotham •where the gates to heaven are forever barred •where evil has declared victory •where hell brushes the earth •where dark demons steal all light

MORE OF MY "PREPARATION," FATHER?

AS I'VE EXPLAINED TO YOU, BRUCE, EVERY DAY OF YOUR LIFE...

SINCE YOUR TRAINING AND STUDIES WILL NEVER STOP SO FAR AS I'M CONCERNED, THEY CAN HARDLY BE DEEMED PREPARATION.

AND AS I'VE ASKED YOU EVERY DAY SINCE I LEARNED TO SPEAK... THEN WHAT IS THE POINT?

IT IS NOT TO PREPARE, BUT TO BE PREPARED-- FOR ANYTHING, AT ANY MOMENT.
YOUR SHERRY, SIR.
THANK YOU, ALFRED.

AND GOING TO THE THEATER TONIGHT...IS PART OF BEING PREPARED?

IT COULD BE, SON.
BUT I PRAY NOT.

ALL RIGHT, FATHER.
BUT I WANT IT ON THE RECORD YET AGAIN...

I RESENT THIS LIFELONG MYSTERY MASQUERADING AS MY LIFE--
--AND IF THE GRAND PLAN ISN'T REVEALED SOON, I MAY WELL LEAVE GOTHAM TO START A REAL LIFE.

DON'T BE ABSURD, BRUCE.
YOU KNOW THAT'S UTTERLY IMPOSSIBLE.

PERHAPS IT IS, MOTHER, BUT WE'LL NEVER KNOW UNLESS I TRY.
YOU CAN'T, BRUCE-- GOTHAM WON'T LET YOU.
NOW GET DRESSED FOR THE THEATER.

GOOD EVENING, LADIES AND GENTLE-MEN...

GOTHAM MEDICAL UNIVERSITY
OPERATING THEATER
TONIGHT:
Dr. EMIL VARNER

OUR SUBJECT HAS BEEN A CORPSE FOR SOME NINE DAYS, AND ITS BRAIN HAS UNDERSTANDABLY SUFFERED SEVERE DAMAGE...

...DETERIORATING TO LITTLE MORE THAN CRANIAL MUSH, AS IT WERE...
IT WILL, NEVERTHELESS, SUFFICE FOR OUR PURPOSES TONIGHT.

WHAT YOU ARE ABOUT TO WITNESS IS A DEMONSTRATION OF POSTMORTEM REANIMATION, THE FIRST IN MEDICAL HISTORY.
KEEP IN MIND, HOWEVER, THAT I PROMISE YOU LIFE...

...NOT MENTAL GYMNASTICS, AND CERTAINLY NOT GENIUS...

...UNLESS, OF COURSE, THE GENIUS IS MINE.
KLATCH
AS FOR OUR DECOMPOSING SUBJECT...

MMMM
BEHOLD! THE CORPSE TWITCHES--
KZZT

MWUHHH
--AND RETURNS FROM THE MYSTERY OF DEATH, AS IF AWAKENING FROM MERE SLEEP!
SPTZZ

BUT YOU SCOFF, SENSING A GROTESQUE CHARADE--NOTHING BUT THE AUTONOMOUS REACTIONS OF BARELY INTACT NERVES, STIMULATED BY ELECTRICAL CURRENT...
FATHER, IT--
STAY CALM, BRUCE.
AND WELL, YOU SHOULD REMAIN SKEPTICAL--BUT WATCH!
HEAR ME, DEAD THING! ARISE!
SPAK KZZT

GET UP AND LIVE!
RUUAHHH
NOW WALK TO ME!

USE THE POWER OF REVERSED DEATH TO KILL YOUR CREATOR!
RAHHH
NYAHRRRRR
--BUT QUICKENED NONETHELESS!
AND YOU SEE, LADIES AND GENTLEMEN OF GOTHAM? VIRTUALLY MINDLESS, OF COURSE, AND BARREN OF ALL SOUL, LONG SINCE FLED...
IT'S... GHASTLY! AS IF THERE AREN'T ENOUGH RESTLESS DEAD IN GOTHAM... NOW SCIENCE ADDS TO THE POPULATION.
YES, MARTHA...
HE HAS FINALLY SUCCEEDED... AND THIS EXPLAINS EVERYTHING.
STUDY HIS FACE, BRUCE--AND REMEMBER IT WELL.
THE CORPSE OR THE SCIENTIST?
THE CORPSE IS NOTHING, BUT DON'T FOOL YOURSELF...
ITS MASTER IS MORE SORCERER THAN SCIENTIST.

NRAAAH
LIFE FROM DEATH— THE FINAL TRIUMPH!

YOU MAY FALL TO YOUR KNEES AND WORSHIP ME AT WILL...
KLATCH
ESPECIALLY YOU, DOCTOR WAYNE.

VOILÀ!
DEATH-- DEAD AGAIN!

DIABOLICAL.

--HARDLY A MERE NIGHT AT THE THEATER, FATHER, NOT WHEN VARNER KNEW YOU.
HE SPOKE DIRECTLY TO YOU--RIGHT FROM THE OPERATING FLOOR.
BELIEVE ME, BRUCE, I NOTICED.

THEN WHEN WILL YOU DISPEL ALL THE MYSTERY AND INITIATE ME?
WHEN WILL YOU TELL ME WHAT'S GOING ON?
WHEN I DO, SON, YOU'LL WISH I HADN'T.

RIGHT INSIDE, SIRS-- ENTERTAINMENT AND ANATOMICAL EDIFICATION! ECDYSIASTS DOWN TO THE SKIN AND BEYOND!
NO COVER CHARGE, NO MINIMUM!
THE BONEYARD
YOU'RE WRONG...

AND LET ME BE THE JUDGE OF WHAT I WISH! LET ME DECIDE--
HEY, BRUCE--I GOT ONE WORD FOR YA...
EH?

WHAT DID YOU SAY?
BATS, BRUCE--BATS.
WH-WHAT IN THE--?

BATSSSSS.
COME ON, SON.
IT'S JUST A GIMMICK TO LURE PEOPLE INTO THE BONEYARD!
EXACTLY MY POINT...

WHY DO WE STAY IN THIS CITY--AMONG TALKING SKELETONS, NO LESS, WHEN ANY NORMAL FAMILY WOULD JUST LEAVE?
BECAUSE GOTHAM IS WHERE HELL BRUSHES THE EARTH--AND WHERE HELL MUST BE STOPPED.

I'VE HEARD THAT A THOUSAND TIMES, FATHER, BUT HOW CAN YOU OR I "STOP HELL"?
ONE DEMON, BRUCE, AT A TIME.

BUT WHAT DOES THAT MEAN?
YOU SKULK AND SCHEME AND STUDY AND GO TO YOUR HUSH-HUSH MEETINGS AS IF YOU'RE ENGAGED IN SOME TOP-SECRET MISSION BUT YOU WON'T LET ME IN!

YOU STILL TREAT ME LIKE A CHILD--SOMETIMES LIKE A SLAVE!
STUDY THIS, MASTER THAT, IT'S "GOOD PREPARATION"--BUT PREPARATION FOR WHAT? WHEN WILL YOU--
STOP IT, BRUCE!

SHOW YOUR FATHER THE RESPECT HE COMMANDS AND TRUST HIS WISDOM--
--WHICH HAS KEPT YOU ALIVE AND FREE ALL THIS TIME.

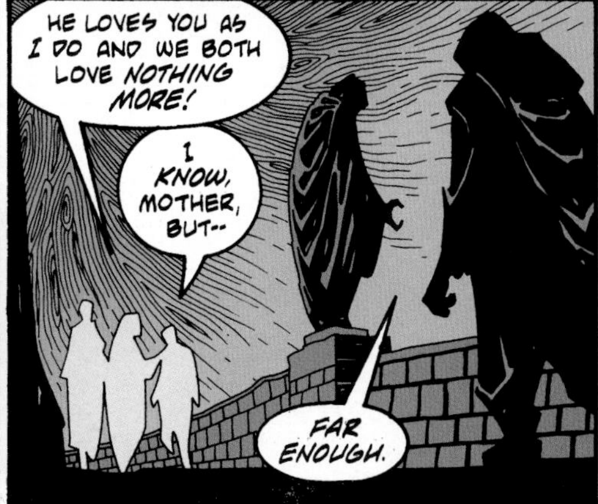
HE LOVES YOU AS I DO AND WE BOTH LOVE NOTHING MORE!
I KNOW, MOTHER, BUT--
FAR ENOUGH.

IT IS TIME, DOCTOR WAYNE, TO GIVE UP THE LAST GHOST.
YOU...!

SKEKT
NO, BRUCE! HE'S--

UHN--!
BRUCE--!
SHUMP

PLASHH

THERE IS MORE THAN ONE WAY, DOCTOR WAYNE, TO HARVEST A GHOST...
RUN, MARTHA-- NOW!
NO, THOMAS! I WILL NOT RUN FROM YOUR DEATH...

IF YOU CANNOT ESCAPE, I WILL NOT.

VERY WELL...AT LEAST OUR SOULS SHALL FLEE TOGETHER.

SUIT YOURSELVES.

ONLY ONE GHOST IS REQUIRED...

-Hwiihh-
-koff a-hukt-
RAOWRRRR
AAAIIEEEE
THE ASSASSIN- MUCH TOO STRONG...
...TOO FAST...
UHRRRRR
NOT NATURAL.
NOT A MAN.

THROATS TORN...

BODIES EVISCERATED...

M-MOTHER...

F-FATHER...

A WEREWOLF.

NOOOOOOOO!

OWROOOOOOOO

ENTER THE BONEYARD, IF YOU DARE!
TONIGHT ONLY, WE PRESENT--

Uhk--!
WHO ARE YOU?
N-NAME'S CAL-- AND NO, BRUCE, NOT FOR CALCIUM, BUT NICE TRY.

YOU SAID "BATS."
ONLY WAY TO FLY, BRUCE, AFTER THE TRASHING OF YOUR PARENTS' SOUL-CONTAINERS.
HOW DO YOU KNOW THEY WERE KILLED?

HEY, EVERY BODY DIES--AND IN GOTHAM ODDS ARE IT'S MURDER.
LAST CHANCE BEFORE I SCATTER YOUR BONES!
WHO ARE YOU?

LIKE YOUR FATHER SAID WHEN HE COULD STILL TALK, I'M MOSTLY A COME-ON FOR THIS CLUB...
BUT THE CREEP WHO PEDDLED ME TO THE OWNER HAD TO EQUIP THESE BONES WITH A SHILL'S PERSONALITY.
AND TO DO THAT, HE HAD TO HIJACK A SHILL'S SOUL--MY SOUL, BRUCE, ONCE ETHER-FREE, NOW CALCIFIED, WOE IS ME.

YOU'RE NOT JUST A TRICK! YOU'RE... DEAD.
I WAS DEAD-- AND WHEN I WAS, I LEARNED THINGS.
LIKE WHAT?

"LIKE PARTS OF THE FUTURE... THE MURDER OF YOUR PARENTS... AND THE NEW LIFE SPAWNED BY THEIR DEATHS... YOUR DESTINY."

WHAT DESTINY?

BATS, BRUCE-- HALFWAY BETWEEN HELL AND THE ONLY HEAVEN YOU'VE EVER KNOWN.

WHAT "HEAVEN" HAVE I--

WAYNE MANOR, BRUCE-- AND STOP GOING SIMPLE ON ME.

THERE'S A LOT OF MISERY IN THIS CURSED CITY, AND WE'RE ALL COUNTING ON YOU.
TO DO WHAT?
WHAT DO YOU WANT TO DO RIGHT NOW? MORE THAN ANYTHING?

"AVENGE THE DEATHS OF MY PARENTS."
"AND THEN?"
GC EMS
AMBULANCE
AMBULANCE
WEREWOLF?
LOOKS LIKE.
"HONOR THEIR LIVES--BY FINISHING THEIR WORK... BY RECLAIMING THE SOUL OF THIS CITY."

INCLUDING MY SOUL, BRUCE.
BUT YOU'RE--
HEY, IT MAY BE FUSED IN BONE OUTSIDE A CLUB FOR NIGHTCRAWLERS, BUT MY SOUL STILL LIVES-- AND IT HAS AN AGENDA.
WHICH IS?
SWEET REVENGE, BABE, ON THE CREEP WHO BROUGHT ME BACK TO LIFE-- MINUS MY FLESH AND BLOOD.
AND WHO DID THAT, "CAL"?

"YOU SAW HIM TONIGHT-- AT THE THEATER WITH YOUR FOLKS."
"DOCTOR EMIL VARNER--?"
"THE SAME."

THEN MAYBE HE IS "MORE SORCERER THAN SCIENTIST"... BUT HOW AM I SUPPOSED TO--
HOW MANY TIMES I GOTTA SAY "BATS," BRUCE?
The BONEYARD
CHECK IT OUT, GENTLEMEN-- LIVE DANCERS!

STEP INSIDE AND SEE 'EM STRIP TO THE SKELETON!
DEATH STOPS NO DANCE IN THE BONEYARD!

ARE YOU ALL RIGHT, MASTER BRUCE?
I CAN FACE THEIR DEATHS, ALFRED... I HAVE NO CHOICE... BUT THERE'S SOMETHING BEYOND THE MURDERS.

WHAT IS IT, SIR?
I... I'M NOT SURE I SHOULD INVOLVE YOU, ALFRED.
AND WHOM ELSE WILL YOU INVOLVE, MASTER BRUCE? THERE ARE NO OTHER MOURNERS-- WE ARE ALONE NOW.

YES, BUT--
I HAVE SERVED YOUR PARENTS WITH UTMOST LOYALTY SINCE SHORTLY AFTER YOUR BIRTH.
I HAVE TUTORED AND TRAINED YOU, HELPED RAISE YOU, ALMOST AS MY OWN SON.
AND NOW, GIVEN THIS TRAGEDY AND WITH YOUR CONSENT, I SHALL SERVE ONLY YOU.

OF COURSE, ALFRED, BUT YOU DON'T KNOW WHAT--
I KNOW FAR MORE THAN YOU SUSPECT, SIR, AND I AM ALREADY INVOLVED.
YOU MAY FURTHER INVOLVE ME AFTER THE BURIAL.

COME, GENTLEMEN, PLEASE-- THE APPROACHING STORM THREATENS ALL LIGHT.
LOWER THE CASKETS BEFORE--

SHRAAAAK--

--KOOOOM

--THE RAIN.
ALFRED, DID YOU SEE--?
MERE GRAVEYARD HAUNTS, MASTER BRUCE.
PAY THEM NO MIND AND--

AHN--!

FATHER--!
DON'T LOOK, MASTER BRUCE...

YOU'VE ALREADY ENDURED TOO MUCH.
CLOSE YOUR EYES AND REMEMBER BETTER TIMES.

GENTLEMEN--WHAT ARE YOU WAITING FOR? RETURN THE DECEASED TO HIS CASKET WITH ALL THE DIGNITY YOU CAN MUSTER!
STORM OR NO STORM, THESE GOOD SOULS WILL BE INTERRED.

THIRTY MINUTES LATER:
"--HALFWAY BETWEEN HELL," HE SAID, "AND THE ONLY HEAVEN YOU'VE EVER KNOWN."

DOES THAT MAKE ANY SENSE TO YOU, ALFRED?
I AM AFRAID IT DOES, SIR.
IT'S ODD THAT THIS "CAL" SKELETON SHOULD KNOW, BUT YOUR DESTINY DOES INDEED LIE--

"--BENEATH WAYNE MANOR."
THIS WAY, SIR...

HERE.
WHERE, ALFRED? YOU'VE LED US TO A DEAD END.
THERE'S NOTHING HERE... OTHER THAN THE GRANDFATHER CLOCK.

KREEEEEK
WHAT THE--?
BEHIND AND BELOW THE CLOCK, SIR...
...HALF-WAY DOWN TO HELL.

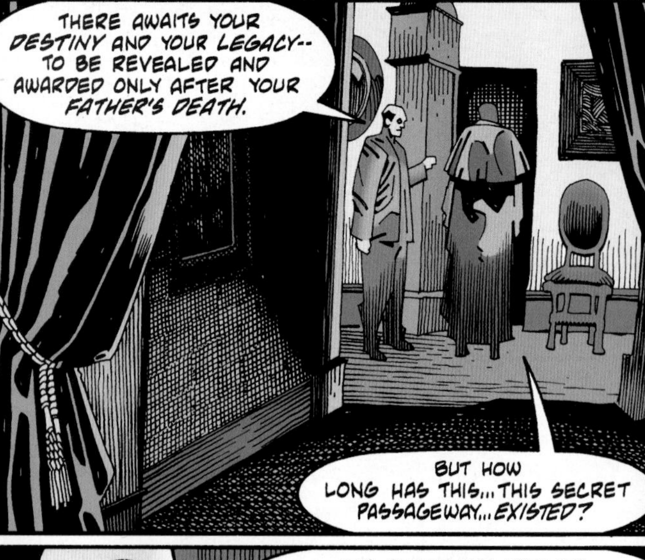
THERE AWAITS YOUR DESTINY AND YOUR LEGACY--TO BE REVEALED AND AWARDED ONLY AFTER YOUR FATHER'S DEATH.
BUT HOW LONG HAS THIS... THIS SECRET PASSAGEWAY... EXISTED?

THE CLOCK WAS HINGED BEFORE I CAME INTO YOUR FATHER'S EMPLOY, SIR, AND SHORTLY AFTER YOU WERE CONCEIVED.
YOU HAVE BEEN PREPARED FOR THIS MOMENT SINCE YOUR BIRTH.
PREPARED BY MY FATHER?
THIS IS WHAT IT WAS ALL ABOUT?

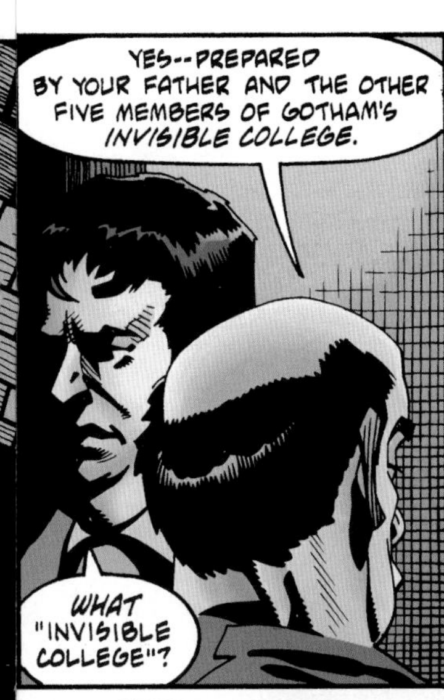
YES--PREPARED BY YOUR FATHER AND THE OTHER FIVE MEMBERS OF GOTHAM'S *INVISIBLE COLLEGE.*
WHAT "INVISIBLE COLLEGE"?

"THEY CALLED THEMSELVES '*THE SECRET SIX,*' SIR, AND THEIR COLLEGE WAS 'INVISIBLE' BECAUSE IT HAD *NO STRUCTURE...*
"THEY MET IN HIDING WHEREVER THEY COULD, TO STUDY AND OPPOSE THE EVIL FORCES POSSESSING GOTHAM."

AND THE OTHER FIVE *ARE*--?

"*DEAD,* I FEAR--SLAIN BY THE *SAME AGENT* WHO MURDERED YOUR PARENTS."

THE *NAMES* OF THE OTHER FIVE?
SECRET EVEN TO *ME,* SIR.
BUT THE NIGHT BEFORE HIS DEATH, YOUR FATHER TOLD ME THE OTHERS HAD BEEN "*ELIMINATED ONE BY ONE.*"
HE WAS THE *LAST OF THE* SECRET SIX.

AND YOU LET HIM *GO OUT*--KNOWING HIS LIFE WAS IN *DANGER* ?!
I *TRIED* TO DISSUADE HIM, SIR... BUT I WAS ORDERED *SILENT.*

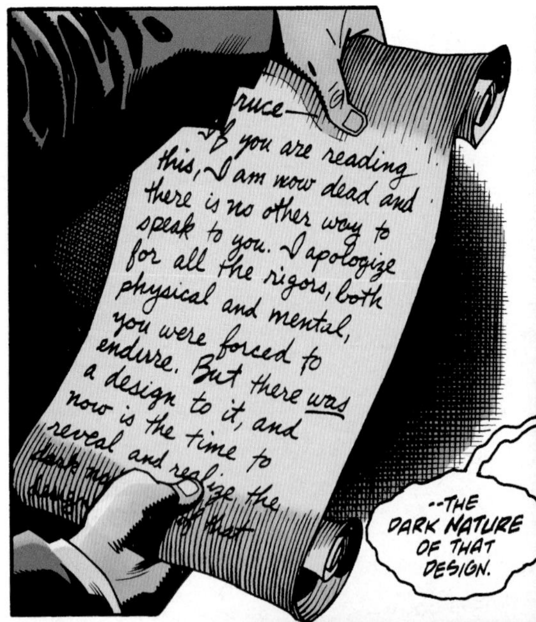
ruce—
If you are reading
this, I am now dead and
there is no other way to
speak to you. I apologize
for all the rigors, both
physical and mental,
you were forced to
endure. But there was
a design to it, and
now is the time to
reveal and realize the
--THE DARK NATURE OF THAT DESIGN.

FATHER! BUT... YOU'RE--
DEAD, YES, BUT NOT UNABLE TO SPEAK TO YOU IN THIS STATE...

I WAS CLEARLY WRONG ABOUT THAT AND PERHAPS MUCH MORE.
IN FACT, IT SEEMS THAT MY DESTINY IS TO... HAUNT YOU.
H-HAUNT ME?

AT LEAST FOR A TIME.
BUT SHOULD YOU SUCCEED ON THE COURSE I'VE CHARTED FOR YOU, I MAY BE ABLE TO... RETIRE... IN PEACE.
MAYBE EVEN FOR ETERNITY... IF THE DARK ONES DON'T CATCH ME FIRST.

WHAT ABOUT MOTHER? WHERE IS--
BETTER YOU SHOULD NOT KNOW, SON.
BUT--
NOT NOW, BRUCE...

TIME IS SHORT AND I'M NOT SURE HOW LONG I CAN SUSTAIN MANIFESTATION.
OPEN THE WOODEN CHEST ON THE STONE ALTAR AND--
AHRRR!
MY-M-MORTAL REMAINS... UNDER ATTACK... GRAVE VIOLATED... AND SOMEONE IS TAKING MY--
--H-HEAD!
FATHER!
WH-WHAT IS HAPPENING TO--
OPEN THE CHEST, SON...
INSIDE YOU WILL FIND... THE DARK DESIGN OF YOUR DESTINY.
WH-WHAT DARK DESIGN...?
IN THE CH-CHEST, BRUCE... PLEASE...
ACCEPT MY LAST GIFT... EMBRACE YOUR FUTURE DESTINY...

AND G-GO TO MY CORPSE BEFORE--

FATHER!

THE GHOST IS GONE--BUT INSIDE THE CHEST...
SOME SORT OF DARK BUNDLE--AND ATOP IT... ANOTHER NOTE.

Gotham's Agents of Evil are a superstitious cabal. Make them fear you.
THIS IS...
INSANE.

ALFRED...
Y-YES, MASTER BRUCE?
I'M GOING OUT.
OF COURSE, SIR, AND I SEE YOU'VE FOUND YOUR DESTINY.
DESIGNED LIKE THIS, ALFRED... IT'S HARD TO MISS.
YOUR FATHER SUGGESTED A VISIT TO POLICE COMMISSIONER JAMES GORDON BEFORE--
NOT YET-- THERE'S SOMETHING MORE PRESSING FIRST.
BUT--
TRUST ME, ALFRED...

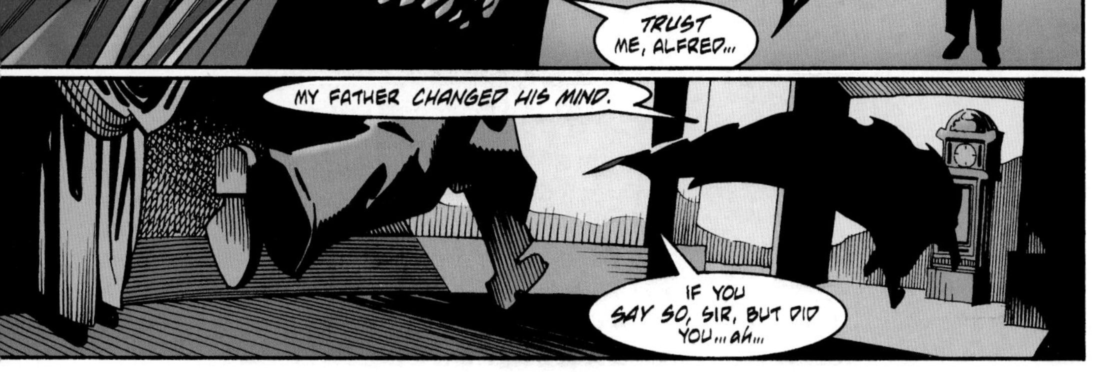

MY FATHER CHANGED HIS MIND.
IF YOU SAY SO, SIR, BUT DID YOU... ah...

"...NOTICE THE CAR?"
VRAOWW
ALSO HARD TO MISS.

SKREEEETCH

ONLY HOURS SINCE THE BURIAL--BUT THE GRAVE'S ALREADY BEEN REOPENED...
DESECRATED.

AND HIS BODY... DEFILED.
THE HEAD... STOLEN...

...JUST AS ITS GHOST TOLD ME.
BUT IF THE WEREWOLF ASSASSIN DID THIS... WHY WAIT UNTIL THE BODY WAS BURIED?

AND IF IT WASN'T THE WEREWOLF?
...THEN WHO DID STEAL MY FATHER'S HEAD?
SEVERE BRAIN DAMAGE OF COURSE...
AND I CERTAINLY DON'T WANT INTELLIGENCE IN MY CREATURE...
...NOT WHEN OBEDIENCE IS FAR MORE IMPORTANT.
...BUT YOUR HEAD, DOCTOR WAYNE, WILL NEVERTHELESS SUFFICE.
ALL I REALLY NEED, YOU SEE, IS YOUR BASIC MOTOR SKILLS.

BUT MOST OF ALL, I NEED ROOM IN THERE FOR ME.
KZZAKT
HAHAH! ONE SPARKED DEATH-RICTUS AND WE'RE LOADED FOR LAUGHS!
IT ALL FITS... ALL THE PIECES FALLING INTO PLACE.
LEFT ARM FROM SYKES... TORSO FROM BRANDT... RIGHT LEG FROM RINCONI... RIGHT ARM FROM JENKINS... LEFT LEG FROM HYNEK... AND HEAD FROM WAYNE...
...ALL ADDING UP TO HORROR.
THE "INVISIBLE COLLEGE," COMMISSIONER GORDON-- WHO WERE THEY? TELL ME ABOUT THE "SECRET SIX."
THE BATMAN, I PRESUME.
BEEN EXPECTING YOU-- ACTUALLY THOUGHT YOU WOULD HAVE BEEN HERE BEFORE NOW.

YOU KNOW ABOUT ME--AND YOU KNEW MY FATHER...
I KNEW THE OTHER FIVE AS WELL--UNTIL ALL SIX OF THEM WERE RECENTLY MURDERED.
WHY?
TO INSTILL FEAR, BATMAN, AND TO CHEAT DEATH.
EVERY GRAVE VIOLATED... A DIFFERENT BODY PART MISSING FROM EACH CORPSE...SIX PUZZLE PIECES FOR A PATCHWORK ATROCITY.

ARE YOU HERE, DARK LORD? IN THE LAB?
IT'S TIME! CAN YOU HEAR ME?

I HEAR YOU, EMIL VARNER.
WELL, MY CORRUPT FLESH WON'T LAST MUCH LONGER, YOU KNOW, AND I DON'T WANT MY FREED SOUL BEING HUNTED AND TORMENTED AND DEVOURED--NOT BY YOU OR ANY OTHER DARK LORD!
AND THAT WAS OUR DEAL, IF YOU'LL RECALL...

SIX MURDERS, SIX SOULS FOR YOU TO HUNT--AND I EVEN THREW IN WAYNE'S WIFE TO MAKE SEVEN.
IN RETURN, YOU GIVE ME THE MEANS TO LIVE ON--AND TO SERVE YOU FURTHER!
Heh.

DO IT, VARNER.
YOUR SCIENCE HAS BEEN AUGMENTED BY OUR SORCERY.
THE TRANSMIGRATION OF YOUR SOUL WILL SUCCEED.
THEN ALLOW ME, DARK LORD, TO SLIP INTO SOMETHING MORE COMFORTABLE...
NAMELY, THE FRESH FLESH OF A NEW BODY--STITCHED TOGETHER FROM SIX OLD ONES!
MY FATHER APPEARED TO ME, COMMISSIONER.
AFTER HIS DEATH?
AS A GHOST, YES.
THEN THE DARK LORDS HAVE NOT YET CAPTURED HIS SOUL.
I'M NOT CERTAIN OF THAT.
HE DEMATERIALIZED... IN DISTRESS.
Huh-- FIFTY-FIFTY, THEN, MAYBE LESS.
HE GAVE ME SOME EXPLANATION, BUT NOT ENOUGH.
THERE MAY BE OTHER LETTERS, A JOURNAL, A DIARY...
I HAVEN'T FULLY EXPLORED THE CAVES YET.
AND YOU WANT ANSWERS-- NOW.
I DEMAND THEM.

VMMMMMM
THE SWITCH IS FLIPPED--AND READY OR NOT...
EOW!
KZZT
SPAK
...HERE I COME!
VZZT SPTZ ZSPRAKT
YESSS! FAREWELL, OLD FLESH!
I'M ALIVE! I'M ALIIIIIVE!
HYAHAHAHAHAAA

KZZT
ZAT
MISMATCHED LEGS, DARK LORD, BUT THEY WORK! I'M WALKING!
THEN TAKE YOUR NEW LIFE, EMIL VARNER... AND FOLLOW THE WAY OF DEATH.
I LIVED A LIE.
MY PARENTS SHAPED ME TOWARD A FORM THEY NEVER REVEALED.
THEIR SERVANT ALFRED PENNYWORTH PARTICIPATED IN IT.
AND YOU KNEW ABOUT IT, COMMISSIONER-- YOU EXPECTED ME.
IT WAS AGREED THAT YOUR FATHER'S DEATH WOULD TRIGGER YOUR CREATION--
--KEPT SECRET UNTIL THEN, HOPING YOU'D GAIN ENOUGH MATURITY TO ACCEPT THE MISSION.
HAVE I?
THAT'S FOR YOU TO PROVE.
YOUR ASSESSMENT?
BLEAK.
NOW THAT THE SIX ARE DEAD, YOU AND I AND PENNYWORTH MAY BE GOTHAM'S ONLY REMAINING HOPE...
...THE ONLY ONES ABLE TO ACT.

"MOST PEOPLE IN THIS CITY SIMPLY ACCEPT THE FACT THAT GOTHAM IS HAUNTED--AND NOBODY FROM THE OUTSIDE TRULY BELIEVES IT...
"...ALTHOUGH THEY'RE IN NO HURRY TO INVESTIGATE.
"OUR CLAIMS ARE DISMISSED AS A TOURISM SCAM--EVEN THOUGH NO TOURISTS DARE VISIT.
"IN FACT, I SUSPECT THERE'S SOME SORT OF SPELL ENSHROUDING THIS ENTIRE CITY..."
Beware all who enter haunted Gotham •where the gates to heaven are forever barred •where evil has declared vict •where hell
THE WORLD KNOWS ABOUT US... WE NEVER APPEAR ON MAPS...BUT SOMEHOW, NO MATTER WHERE AN OUTSIDER IS GOING, THERE'S A DETOUR WHEN WE'RE IN THE WAY.
WE'RE ALONE HERE, A SELF-CONTAINED CITY POSSESSED BY DARK FORCES.
YOU'RE EXAGGERATING.
OH? AND HAVE YOU EVER TRIED TO LEAVE?
UNTIL NOW, I'VE HAD TO STAY--WITH MY PARENTS...
THAT'S THE USUAL EXCUSE.
"WHO WOULD TAKE CARE OF MY CHILD? WHAT WOULD MY MOTHER DO?"--AS IF NO ONE EVER HEARD OF A FAMILY MOVING AWAY.
IT JUST DOESN'T OCCUR TO THEM--IT'S NOT AN OPTION--AND YOU KNOW WHY?
"BECAUSE GOTHAM IS HELL'S HUNTING GROUND, STOCKED WITH PREY--AND WE'RE IT."
DID YOU HEAR SOMETHING?
N-NO, BUT... THERE'S A SHADOW AHEAD!

THAT'S... ABSURD.
THEN GO OUT TO THE CITY LIMITS--AND TRY TO CROSS THE LINE.
PLENTY OF--

YES, CERTAIN PEOPLE CAN AND DO--THE ONES ALLOWED PASSAGE...
...BUT ONLY TO RUN ERRANDS FOR THE POWERS THAT BE--POWERS WE ALL SUFFER BUT TAKE IN STRIDE WITHOUT EVEN THINKING ABOUT IT.

BUT YOU DO THINK ABOUT IT, COMMISSIONER.
HOW IS THAT?
CALL IT... MENTAL YOGA.
I WAS "ENLIGHTENED"... AFTER GOING TO COLLEGE.
THE INVISIBLE COLLEGE?
YOU'RE LOOMING OVER THE SECRET SEVENT, FAR MORE SECRET THAN THE OTHER SIX.

TOO SECRET TO ATTEND AN ACTUAL MEETING... OR EVEN YOUR PARENTS' FUNERAL.
BUT YOU'VE ATTENDED THE COLLEGE YOUR WHOLE LIFE.
WITHOUT KNOWING IT.

MAYBE NOT, BUT YOU JUST GRADUATED--WITH HONORS.
WHY ME?
BECAUSE YOU'RE THE PROGENY OF A GREAT MAN AND A GREAT WOMAN...

BECAUSE THEY'RE DEAD NOW.
BECAUSE YOU AND I AND PENNYWORTH ARE THE ONLY ONES LEFT...
...AND TWO OF US ARE OLD.
YOUR FATHER PREFERRED "THE BATMAN."
BUT WHY A BAT?
CREATURE OF THE NIGHT... MYSTERIOUS... FRIGHTENING...
THEN I WAS DESIGNED FROM BIRTH-- TO SOMEDAY STAND HERE AS... THIS.
AND YOU EVEN HAVE A NAME FOR ME-- "BATMAN."
IT WAS ALL VERY CALCULATED-- A PLAN FOR FIGHTING FIRE WITH FIRE, GIVING THE DARK LORDS A DOSE OF THEIR OWN NASTY MEDICINE.
ALSO, YOUR FATHER RECEIVED SOME KIND OF "SIGN," ALTHOUGH HE NEVER GAVE ME DETAILS...
MAYBE IN TIME, THEY'LL BE REVEALED TO YOU.
TELL ME... WAS MY FATHER A SORCERER?
A MYSTIC, MAYBE--AN OCCULT SCHOLAR, DEFINITELY--BUT A SORCERER, NEVER!
THE DARK ARTS ARE THE VERY SOURCE OF GOTHAM'S DAMNATION-- AND YOUR FATHER LOATHED THEM.
WITH A PASSION.

HREHRR

I **DID** IT! THE FOOLS THOUGHT I WAS **JOKING**, BUT THE JOKE'S ON **THEM**-- ALL **SIX** OF THEM!

HYAH!

IN FACT, THE JOKE'S **IN** THEM--OR AT LEAST IN THEIR DISMEMBERED AND REASSEMBLED **PARTS!**

AND THE JOKE IS **IMMORTAL!** I CAN LIVE **FOREVER** NOW!

I CAN **SERVE** YOU FOREVER, DARK LORDS OF GOTHAM--**FEED** YOU FOREVER!

AND BELIEVE ME, I SHALL TAKE **HUGE AMUSEMENT** IN THE ONGOING PROCESS HYAHAHAHAHAAA!

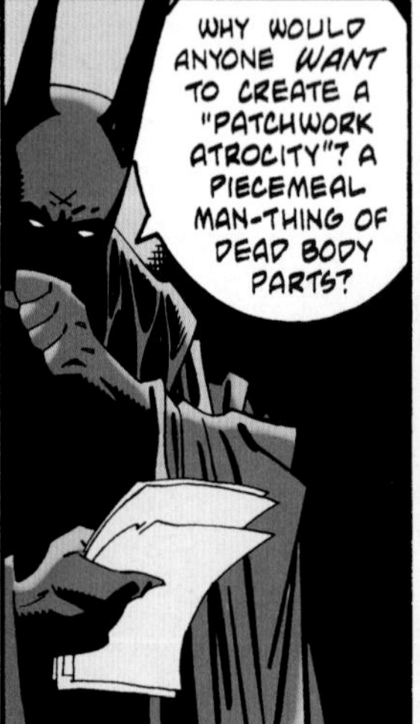
WHY WOULD ANYONE *WANT* TO CREATE A "PATCHWORK ATROCITY"? A PIECEMEAL MAN-THING OF DEAD BODY PARTS?

TO MAKE IT *LIVE*, I'D GUESS-- LIKE *DOCTOR FRANKENSTEIN.*

Hmmm.
AND WHO WOULD *THAT* BE?

THAT I *DON'T* KNOW.

BUT MAYBE I DO, GORDON...
YOU DO--?
...AND CAL MAY GET HIS "SWEET REVENGE" AFTER ALL.
"CAL"? WHO THE DEVIL --?
DOCTOR EMIL VARNER...
Huh--?
HE LIVES IN THIS BUILDING.
WHAT FLOOR?
WH-WHO ARE YOU?
THE BATMAN.
P-PLEASE--I GOT KIDS...
THEN TREAT THEM WELL--AND YOU NEED NEVER FEAR ME.

WH-
WHAT ARE
YOU?
A
PREDATOR--
BUT ONE WHO
PREYS ONLY ON
EVIL.
WHAT
FLOOR FOR
VARNER?
F-F-FIFTH.

MY FATHER
WAS RIGHT.
THE BAT-IMAGE
DOES INSPIRE
FEAR--BUT I
WILL PREY ON
NOTHING HERE...

VARNER
IS ALREADY
DEAD.
APPARENTLY
ELECTROCUTED.

BUT WHERE IS
MY FATHER'S
HEAD?
WHERE ARE THE
GRAVEROBBED PIECES
OF THE OTHER FIVE?

AND WHO
KILLED
VARNER?
BEHIND
THIS
DOOR...?

RAHRRR!

THE WEREWOLF!

THE ASSASSIN!

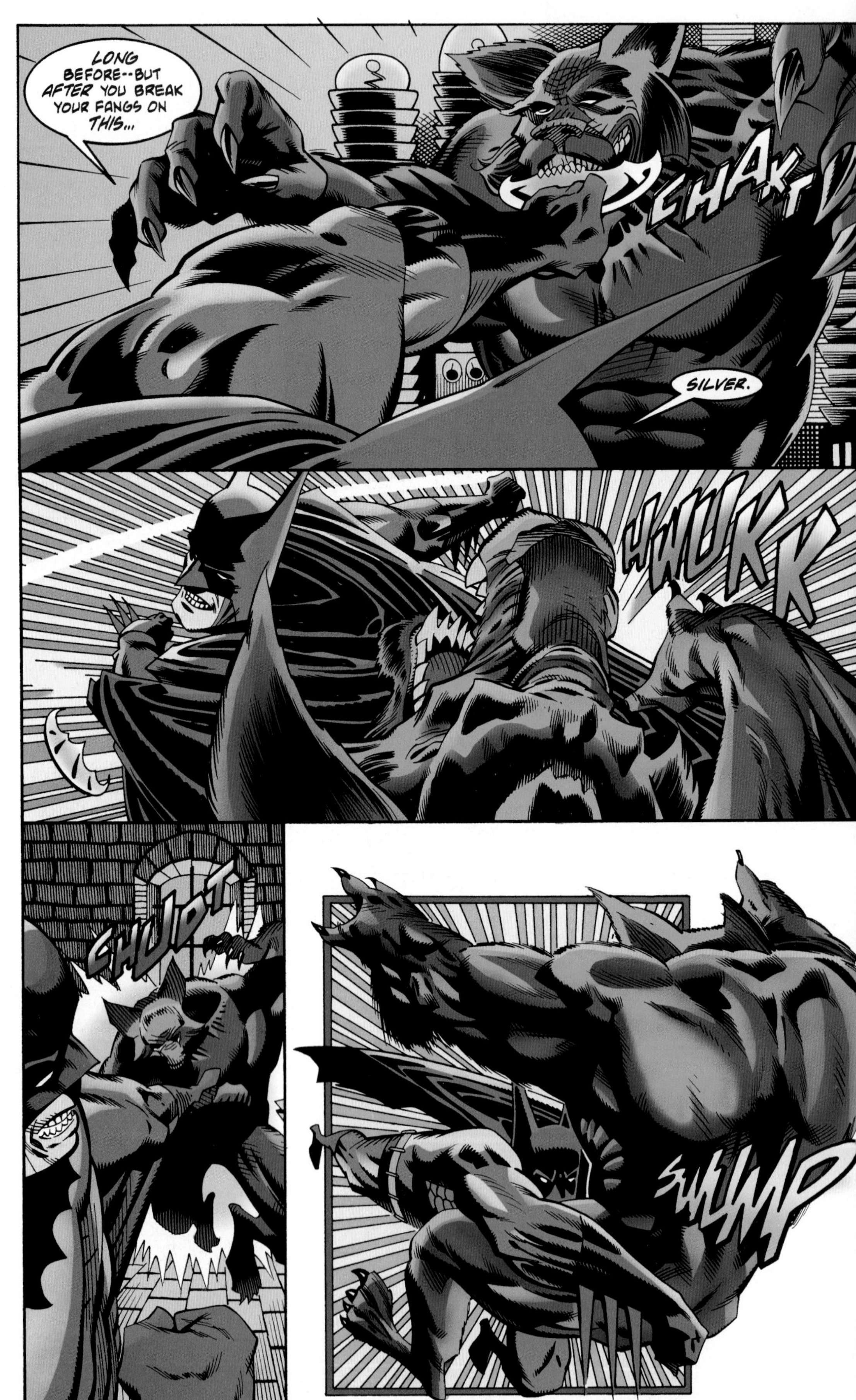
LONG BEFORE--BUT AFTER YOU BREAK YOUR FANGS ON THIS...
CHAKT
SILVER.
HWUKK
CHUDT
SHUMP

BLASHH
WHAT THE--?
FIRST A GRIN IN STITCHES...
THEN A "BAT-MAN"...
WUMPT
SWUDD
AND NOW A WEREWOLF!
BAM BAM BAM
BAM

BAM
BAM
ALREADY SPRINTING--
AND NO WAY I CAN
MATCH HIS SPEED.
SORRY I COULDN'T PUT THE BEAST DOWN, BUT A DOORMAN'S SALARY DOESN'T COVER SILVER BULLETS--NOT WITH KIDS TO FEED.
AT LEAST I SCARED HIM OFF.
AND I MAY NEVER FIND HIM AGAIN.
HUH--?
NEVER MIND--YOU TRIED TO DO RIGHT.
ANYONE UNUSUAL LEAVE THIS BUILDING TONIGHT?
YEAH, A REAL FREAK--CREEPED ME OUT MORE'N YOU, AT FIRST GLANCE ANYWAY...
STITCHES EVERYWHERE--LOOKED LIKE HE CAME FROM A TRAIN WRECK, EXCEPT FOR THIS BIG, FAT, FULL-FACE GHASTLY GRIN.
ACTED LIKE HE KNEW ME, BUT I NEVER SEEN A MESS LIKE THAT BEFORE--AND BELIEVE ME, I'D REMEMBER.
ANYTHING ELSE?
SAID HE WAS "NO JOKER"--AND HE WAS GONNA MAKE "ALL HELL BUST LOOSE."
BUT HE WAS LAUGHIN' LIKE A LUNATIC, SO I DIDN'T REALLY TAKE HIM SERIOUS--BUT YOU, MAN, YOU'RE AS SERIOUS AS A SORCERER'S SPELL.
YOU TOOK ON A WEREWOLF--
--AND YOU'RE STILL STANDIN'!
SO IS THE WEREWOLF.

YEAH, BUT... YOU RODE THAT THING DOWN A FIVE-FLOOR DROP AND CAME UP FIGHTIN'.
I'M MORE SERIOUS THAN YOU KNOW.
I WOULD HAVE WON.

MY SUSPECT'S DEAD, GORDON-- POSSIBLY MURDERED BY THE SAME ASSASSIN.
YOU MEAN THE WEREWOLF?

YES, ALTHOUGH ELECTROCUTION HARDLY FITS A WEREWOLF'S STYLE.
PLUS THERE'S A WILD CARD...
LEFT THE SCENE CALLING HIMSELF A "JOKER"--AND FITTING YOUR NOTION OF A "PATCHWORK ATROCITY."

BROUGHT TO LIFE--SO OUR "DOCTOR FRANKENSTEIN" COULD HAVE BEEN ELECTROCUTED BY HIS OWN MONSTER.
WHO WAS HE?
RIGHT BEFORE THEIR DEATHS, MY PARENTS TOOK ME TO A SCIENTIFIC DEMONSTRATION--THE REANIMATION OF A CORPSE.

THE SCIENTIST KNEW MY FATHER.
EMIL VARNER? IT'S HIM?
WAS HIM, COMMISSIONER.
VARNER'S DEAD NOW.

MAYBE HIS BODY IS DEAD, BUT IT'S BEEN HEADING THAT WAY FOR YEARS.
CANCER-- AND HE DIDN'T HAVE LONG TO GO.
HE WASN'T ELECTROCUTED--HE SIMPLY NEEDED A NEW BODY.
YOU'RE SAYING VARNER IS STILL ALIVE?
WHY ELSE ROB THOSE GRAVES-- IF NOT TO TRANSFER HIS MIND AND SOUL INTO A NEW PATCHWORK FORM?
VINDICATION, TRIUMPH, MAYBE ETERNAL LIFE, AND REVENGE ON HIS FORMER COLLEAGUES... ALL AT THE MERE COST OF SIX MURDERS--SEVEN, COUNTING YOUR MOTHER.
FORMER COLLEAGUES--?
VARNER WAS ALSO A MEMBER OF THE INVISIBLE COLLEGE...
...BEFORE HE WAS THROWN OUT FOR "DARING TO PLAY GOD"-- AND TRYING TO ENHANCE HIS SCIENCE BY POLLUTING IT WITH THE SUPERNATURAL.
AND NOW HE'S SUCCEEDED?
THAT'S MY GUESS.
EMIL VARNER IS STILL ALIVE AND LAUGHING--WITHIN THE PROFANED AND RESURRECTED FLESH OF THE SECRET SIX.

VMMMMM

MMMMMM

COME ON, WHAT ARE YOU WAITING FOR? YOUR GRAVES ARE JUICED!

BREAK THE DIRT, DEAD THINGS! RISE AND ROT!

HYEEH!

ZZZT
SPAK
FRAZZ

YES! THAT'S MORE LIKE IT--HYAHAHA! ANIMATION--WITHOUT TRANSMIGRATION.

NOW IT'S TIME TO RELEASE NEW AND FAR MORE SUCCULENT SOULS!
GO--AND KILL, KILL, KILL!
HYAHAHAHAHAHAAA!

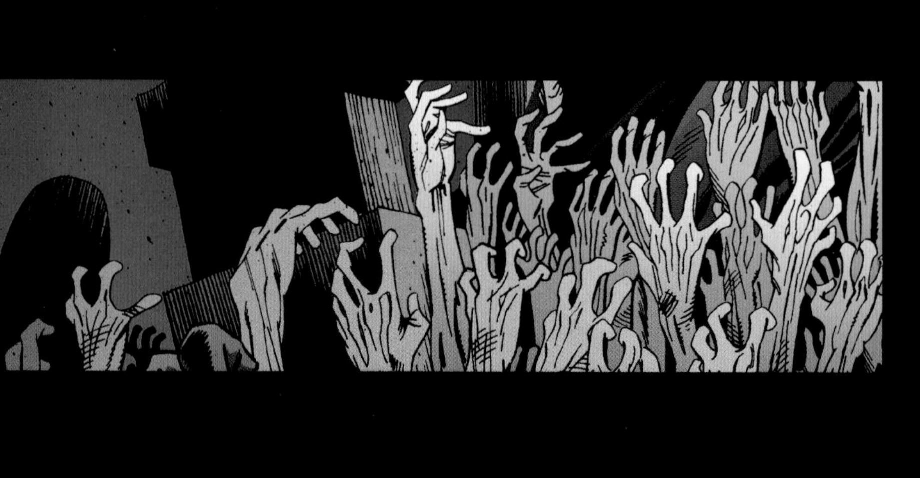

HAUNTED GOTHAM
NIGHT CREATURES
PART TWO
YOU WANT ME TO EXORCISE GOTHAM, COMMISSIONER GORDON, BUT I WAS TRAINED TO BE AN ATHLETE AND A FIGHTER, A DETECTIVE AND A STRATEGIST.
I POSSESS NO POWERS.
I AM NOT SUPERNATURAL.
PRECISELY.
UNLIKE MOST OF THE THINGS HAUNTING THIS CITY, YOU HAVE TO LOOK DARK WITHOUT BEING DARK.
TO FIGHT FOR THE SOULS OF PEOPLE, YOU'LL HAVE TO REMAIN HUMAN.
YOU CAN'T BE A REAL BAT-MAN.
YOU CAN ONLY WEAR THAT COSTUME.

SHOULD YOU EVER BECOME A TRUE CREATURE OF THE NIGHT, IT'S ALL OVER.
YOU'LL BE THE ENEMY--ONE OF THEM.
AND IF I REMAIN "PURE"... BUT THEY SIMPLY KILL ME?
AGAIN, IT'S OVER.
ON OUR OWN, ALFRED PENNYWORTH AND I WOULDN'T STAND A CHANCE.
AND MY DEATH WOULD BE--
THE END OF SUFFERING FOR YOUR FLESH, BUT ONLY THE BEGINNING OF TORMENT FOR YOUR SOUL...
"...WHEN THE DARK LORDS HUNT IT DOWN-- TO PERVERT AND DEVOUR IT."
HEAR ME, DEAD THINGS!
WE SERVE THE DARK LORDS NOW--AND THEY HUNGER!
GO! SHAMBLE FORTH FROM YOUR GRAVES TO KILL THE LIVING!
FREE THE BEST SOULS YOU FIND--AND LET THE FEEDING FRENZY FROTH!
HYAHAHAHAHAA

TOUGH CHOICE--
DARKNESS IN LIFE... OR WORSE IN DEATH.
COMMISSIONER GORDON
IN
OUT
EASIER, ON BALANCE, TO JUST GIVE IN.
"IF YOU CAN'T BEAT 'EM, JOIN 'EM."
NEVER, COMMISSIONER.
NO? WITH YOUR TRAINING, YOUR BACKGROUND... YOU MIGHT BE ONE OF THE FEW OFFERED ACTUAL MEMBERSHIP.
HELL OF A CLUB.
YES, BUT GIVEN THE ALTERNATIVE, I WOULDN'T BLAME YOU FOR ACCEPTING.
INK
THAT'S WHY I WAS SKEPTICAL ABOUT THIS WHOLE BAT GAMBIT--WHY IT WAS THE SOURCE OF GREAT ARGUMENT BETWEEN YOUR FATHER AND ME.
BUT NOW THAT HE'S DEAD, YOU'RE WILLING TO GO ALONG WITH THIS PLAN? WILLING TO BE MY... WHAT? PARTNER?
THAT'S MY TOUGH CHOICE.
I'M POLICE COMMISSIONER OF THIS CURSED CITY--YET I CAN'T PROTECT A SOUL, NOT REALLY...
I NEED HELP--AND BIG HELP.
SOMEONE JUST LIKE "THE BATMAN"... PROVIDED YOU CAN HAUNT THE SHADOWS WITHOUT GETTING DARK.
BUT DON'T FLATTER YOURSELF, NOT YET...

MORE FEARSOME THAN A DEMON, BUT SWORN ENEMY TO SAME... A FORCE FOR GOOD, CHAMPION OF UNDERDOG INNOCENTS... DARK GUARDIAN OF GOTHAM'S SOUL...
BUT... I HAVEN'T DONE ANYTHING YET.

SURE YOU HAVE.
YOU'VE AGREED TO DRESS UP LIKE A BAT AND PLAY THE ROLE.
BUT... I HAVEN'T REALLY DONE ANYTHING.
AND MAYBE YOU WON'T.

MAYBE YOU'LL JUST DIE--GIVE UP THE GHOST...
FREE YOUR SOUL TO FLEE OR FEED A DEMON.
BUT PRESS RELEASES ARE CHEAP AND THEY DON'T HAVE TO BE TRUE.
I'VE ALREADY LEAKED SOME OF THESE PREPARED IN ADVANCE BY THE SIX, MOSTLY YOUR FATHER.

LURID STUFF, BUT ODDLY COMPELLING.
YOU'LL BE A LEGEND IN NO TIME, GIVING THE ENEMY SOMETHING TO THINK ABOUT.

IN THE MEANTIME, STUDY THOSE SIX MURDER REPORTS.
TRY TO REMEMBER IF YOUR FATHER EVER SAID ANYTHING THAT MIGHT BE A CLUE.

WE NEED TO KNOW WHO AMPLIFIED EMIL VARNER'S SCIENCE WITH THE POWER OF SORCERY--AND HOW HE WAS ABLE TO BECOME THIS PATCHWORK "JOKER."
THAT'S THE QUESTION...

"WHO ENABLED HIM TO BRING DEATH BACK TO LIFE? AND WHY?"

MOMMY, WHY DON'T WE LEAVE GOTHAM?
IT'S JUST... NOT POSSIBLE, DEAR.
NOW HUSH AND TRY TO SLEEP.

JOHN? WHY DON'T WE... WHY DON'T WE TRY?
Hm?

TRY WHAT?
TRY TO... TO GET OUT.
OH, NOT THAT AGAIN.
Gotham Gazette
MYSTERIOUS BAT-MAN SLAYS DEMONS
YOU KNOW VERY WELL WE CAN'T--

BASHHH
Z-ZOMBIE--!

WAYNE MANOR:

NOTHING IN THE REPORTS THAT EVEN LINKS THE VICTIMS-- OTHER THAN THE OBVIOUS MARRIAGE OF MY PARENTS.

NO INDICATION THAT THE OTHERS EVER MET, LET ALONE COLLABORATED IN AN "INVISIBLE COLLEGE" TO STUDY AND OPPOSE GOTHAM'S EVIL.

AND I CAN'T REMEMBER ANYTHING CLOSE TO A CLUE, FROM MY FATHER OR MOTHER.
NOTHING SPECIFIC, ANYWAY-- JUST GENERAL TRAINING AND OVERALL TEACHING.
MAYBE I SHOULD GO OUT AGAIN--AS THE BATMAN-- SHOW MYSELF IN UNDERWORLD HAUNTS, TRY TO STIR UP--

BRUUMMMM

W-WHAT...?

BRUMMMMM
KRAKT
SKEEE

EARTHQUAKE-- EMANATING FROM THE BAT ALTAR...!

HARDER TO CROSS OVER... BUT MUST GIVE WARNING...
FATHER? TRAPPED IN THE STONE BAT?
THE EVIL MUST BE CONFRONTED ON ITS OWN TERMS BY A RIGHTEOUS FORCE CLOAKED IN DARKNESS USING FEAR AGAINST FEAR.
BUT NOT USING THE DARK ARTS?
NEVER! YOUR POWER MUST BE NATURAL AND SELF-MADE.
YOU MUST STAND IN OPPOSITION TO THE DARK LORDS, NOT IN CONCERT.

THAT'S WHAT GORDON SAID, BUT I MUST SURRENDER TO THE DARKNESS--AT LEAST PSYCHOLOGICALLY...
...TO GAIN THE POWER TO OPPOSE THEM.
IT IS A RISK, AND THE SEDUCTION WILL BE TEMPTING...

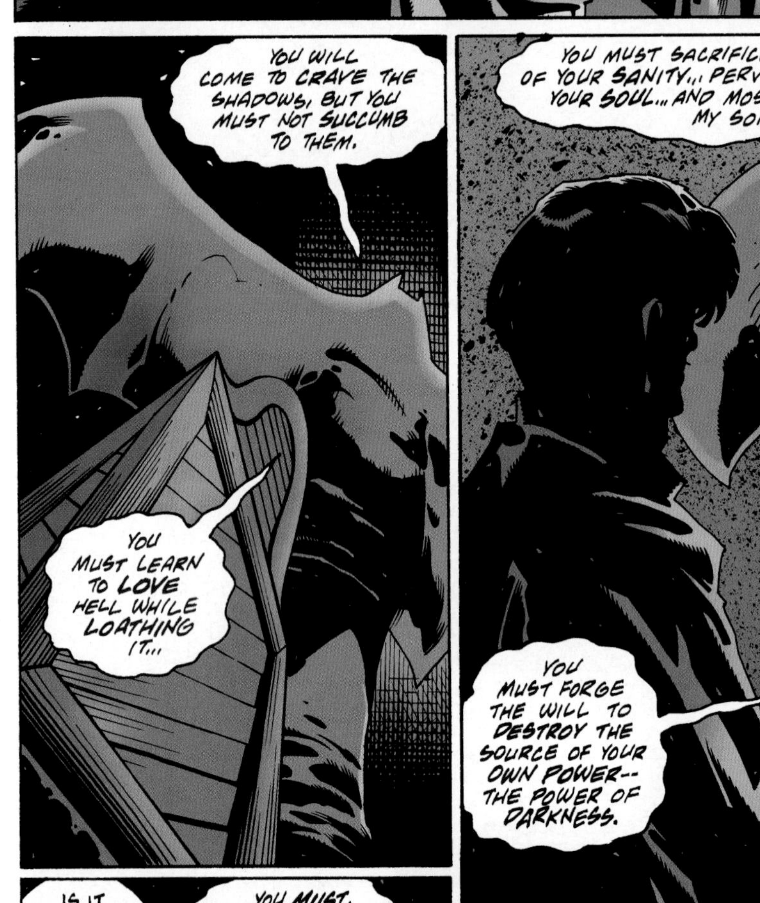
YOU WILL COME TO CRAVE THE SHADOWS, BUT YOU MUST NOT SUCCUMB TO THEM.
YOU MUST LEARN TO LOVE HELL WHILE LOATHING IT...
YOU MUST SACRIFICE A MEASURE OF YOUR SANITY... PERVERT A PORTION OF YOUR SOUL... AND MOST IMPORTANT, MY SON...
YOU MUST FORGE THE WILL TO DESTROY THE SOURCE OF YOUR OWN POWER-- THE POWER OF DARKNESS.

IS IT POSSIBLE, FATHER? HAVE YOU PREPARED ME WELL ENOUGH? CAN I DO IT?
YOU MUST, BRUCE, ALTHOUGH THE EFFORT MAY DESTROY YOU.

TO REDEEM THIS CITY, YOU MUST RISK PERSONAL DAMNATION.
TO FACE AND FIGHT THE TERROR, YOU MUST BECOME TERROR... EVER FIGHTING YOURSELF.

AND NOW, MY SON... TEND YOUR LEFT HAND.
Eh--?

STONE SHARD... FROM THE SHATTERED STALACTITE...

AND THE BLOOD...
BOTH BITTER AND SWEET...

I UNDERSTAND, FATHER.
AND YOU HAVE PREPARED ME WELL.

I CAN WEAR THIS CLOAK OF DARKNESS...
I CAN ENTER THE SHADOWS-- WITHOUT BEING CONSUMED...

"AND I CAN PROTECT THE INNOCENTS OF GOTHAM."
I'M TELLING YOU I HEARD SOMETHING, GEORGE.
LIKE WHAT?
I DON'T KNOW-- SOMETHING OUTSIDE, LIKE MAYBE A SCREAM OR--
SHASH
AUH-K!
YAIEEEEEEEEEEEE
NO--!
Gotham News
BAT-MAN FOILS POLTERGEIST ATTACK

MY WIFE! PUT HER DOWN! PUT HER--

WHUMF

STREET OF THE LIVING-BUT-SOON-TO-BE-DEAD!
HOUSE BY HOUSE, ZOMBIE-GRUNTS, ONE FAMILY AFTER ANOTHER...
CRASH AND CRUSH!
HYEEHAHAHAHAHAAA

I SAID CHECK.
I'M THINKIN', I'M THINKIN'.
ME TOO, AND ON SECOND THOUGHT, IT'S CHECK AND--

PRUTCH
KRUTCH
--MATE?
PRURT
EEEYAAAAHHH

TUMP TUMP TUMP
GO AWAY! WE DON'T WANT ANY!
JUST LEAVE US--
SKRAKAKASH
OH NO-- Z-ZOMBIE...
NYAHRRR
HAHA HAHAA HAA
TAKE THEM ALL!
KILL, KILL, KILL!!

MASTER BRUCE --?
I BELIEVE YOU ARE BEING SUMMONED, SIR--AS THE BAT.

"SUMMONED," ALFRED?
ON THE PHONE?

AH, NO...
BY THE POWER OF LIGHT, SIR... APPARENTLY BEAMING FROM--

"--POLICE HEADQUARTERS."
GLAD YOU GOT THE MESSAGE.
NOT MANY PEOPLE LOOK UP IN THIS TOWN.

YOU CAN THANK ALFRED, COMMISSIONER.
HE SELDOM HANGS HIS HEAD.
BUT YOU HAVE TROUBLE?
REPORTS OF ZOMBIES.
ON A KILLING SPREE IN THE BLACKFRIAR DISTRICT...

NONE OF MY PEOPLE WILL *TOUCH* IT-- WON'T EVEN RESPOND TO THE *CALL*, I'M ASHAMED TO SAY.
DON'T BE, GORDON-- NOT IF IT'S *ZOMBIES*.

ANY CONNECTION TO *EMIL VARNER?*
NOTHING SOLID, BUT IF VARNER TRANSFERRED HIS SOUL INTO THE STITCHED-TOGETHER PIECES OF SIX CORPSES, HE'S A *"JIGSAW ZOMBIE" HIMSELF--*

BUT ONE WITH *FREE WILL.*
STILL ABLE TO *THINK*, MAYBE CONTROL *OTHERS.*
I'LL GO TO BLACKFRIAR AND *CHECK IT OUT.*
ANYTHING NEW ON THE *WEREWOLF ASSASSIN?*

NOT YET.
I'VE GOT AN UNDERCOVER OFFICER ON IT *NOW*--ONE OF THE FEW GUTSY COPS LEFT ON THE *FORCE.*
IF YOU SURVIVE THE *ZOMBIES,* STOP BACK AND--

Eh--? GONE AGAIN...
SILENT AS A *GHOST.*

the CRIPPLED VAMPIRE
"WELL, I DON'T KNOW, JARED... WHY THE BACK ROOM?"
MORE PRIVATE, MORE FUN.
OH, REALLY?
STORAGE
BUT ARE WE TALKING FIRST DATE KIND OF FUN?
AN EXPERIENCE, CASSIE, UNLIKE ANY YOU'VE EVER HAD.
THAT'S WHAT I'M AFRAID OF, JARED... BUT I GUESS I'M ALSO GAME.
INDEED, SSIE--AND TRUST ME...
THE DINING WILL BE DELICIOUS.
WHOA.
UH... JARED? WHY DO ALL THESE PEOPLE LOOK SO... UM... EAGER?

BECAUSE THEY'RE HUNGRY, CASSIE...

...AND WE'RE NOT PEOPLE.
Uhrrr
THEN YOU'VE LED ME TO THE JACKPOT, JARED...

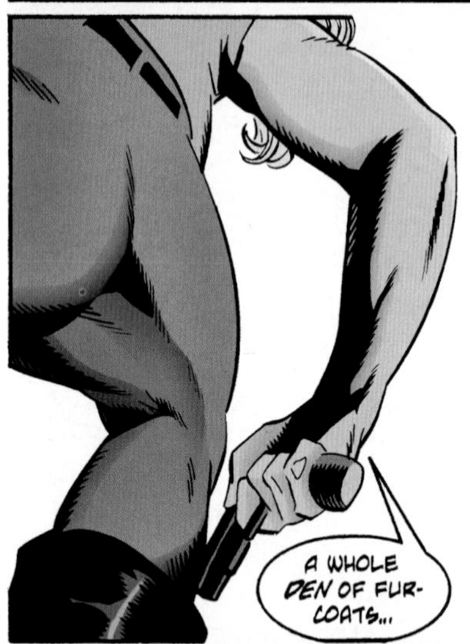
A WHOLE DEN OF FUR-COATS...

...JUST AS I SUSPECTED WHEN YOU CAME ON LIKE THE BIG BAD WOLF.
UNDERCOVER POLICE!
YOU'VE GOT FIVE SECONDS TO FREEZE YOUR TRANSFORMATIONS AND REVERT TO HUMAN!

RUURRRRRR
AROOOOO
ONE... TWO...

FIVE!
RAIK
RAOWRR
BAM BAM
AND TO HELL WITH THREE AND FOUR!

FEELING PAIN, SHAPESHIFTERS?
TRY TO EAT ME AND YOU FEAST ON A MOTHER LODE OF SILVER BULLETS!
BAMBAMBAM

THE BLACKFRIAR AREA...
N-NO... P-PLEASE...
...AND GORDON WAS RIGHT.

THIS WHOLE STREET IS INFESTED WITH ZOMBIES.
Huh--?
S-SAVED ...?
STFT

YOU'RE DEAD, ZOMBIE...
ACT LIKE IT!
SWUKT
IT'S... THE BAT-MAN...FROM THE NEWSPAPERS!
THEY'RE SURROUNDING ME, BUT I FEEL NO FEAR.
I'M STILL RAW IN THIS NEW ROLE...
AGH!
...BUT I'M READY...
...MY ENTIRE LIFE BLINDLY POINTED TO THIS MOMENT.
KRETCH

THIS IS WHAT I'VE STUDIED AND TRAINED FOR...
SPLUTCH
...WITHOUT KNOWING IT.
KRUFT
THIS IS THE DESIGN OF MY DARK DESTINY...
SH-KLK
FROOOSH
...A FINAL FORM AND FURY NEVER EVEN **SUSPECTED.**
A **BAT**-MAN... AND HE'S **REAL?**
SCOURGE OF DARKNESS...

BANE OF EVIL.

AND NOT JUST REAL...
...BUT A FLAMING TERROR!

A LIFE OF MEANINGLESS MYSTERY, PREPARATION OF SHAPELESS INTENT, NOW SOLIDIFIED TO MAKE **PERFECT SENSE**-- AS GOTHAM'S NEW DEFENDER, THE BAT.

OVER HERE! I'M LIFE--RIGHT OUT IN THE OPEN!
COME AND TAKE IT!

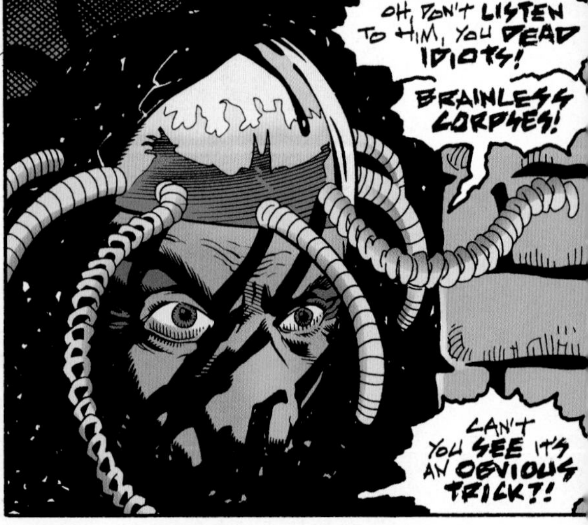

OH, DON'T LISTEN TO HIM, YOU DEAD IDIOTS!
BRAINLESS CORPSES!
CAN'T YOU SEE IT'S AN OBVIOUS TRICK?!

AND BEST OF ALL, THANKS TO MY FATHER'S WISDOM AND SECRECY...

...I SEEM TO SPRING FORTH FROM NOTHING--A CREATURE BORN OF THE NIGHT AND ITS SHADOWS.

THAT'S RIGHT, KEEP COMING!

CONVERGE ON ME...

CH-KLETCH
deetdeetdeet
...BUT EAT THIS!

A SINGLE GRENADE--
TAK
KLAK
TAKT

--FOR ALL OF THEM.
BWHOOOM

Heh.
THE DARK LORDS WILL NOT BE AMUSED!

OVERKILL, MAYBE...
BUT THEIR FIRST DEATHS DIDN'T TAKE.
AND NOW...

NOT EVEN A TWITCH REMAINS.

GORDON IS PLEASED, BUT WHO IS--
WANT YOU TO MEET SOMEONE--THE UNDERCOVER OFFICER I MENTIONED...
CASSANDRA KNIGHT, THIS IS THE BATMAN.

NOT BAD, COMMISH--MAYBE EVEN CLOSE TO HIS PHONY PRESS.
I DON'T FRIGHTEN YOU?
YOU'VE GOT SOMETHING... BUT AFTER WHAT I'VE BEEN THROUGH, IT'S NOTHING.

CASSANDRA PENETRATED A CELL OF WEREWOLVES--FIRST COP TO ESCAPE UNBITTEN.
UNSCRATCHED--AFTER DRILLING SILVER THROUGH TWO OF THEM...

AND THEY CALL THEMSELVES A DEN OR A PACK, COMMISH, NOT A "CELL."
INCLUDING THE ASSASSIN?

ONE OF THEM HAD A SCAR...
HERE.

JUST LIKE THE SHAPE-SHIFTER ASSASSIN.
IT IS TIME, DOCTOR WAYNE, TO GIVE UP THE LAST GHOST.
WHERE IS HE, OFFICER KNIGHT?

I'LL SHOW YOU.
I'M GOING ALONE.
GORDON'S ALL THE PARTNER I NEED--AND I WANT NO COMPANY.

HE'S ONE OF US, OFFICER KNIGHT.
TELL HIM.
PLACE CALLED "THE CRIPPLED VAMPIRE."
IN THE KNIFEHEAD AREA--OFF DANTE'S ALLEY NEAR BLOOD RIVER.

the CRIPPLED VAMPIRE
MOVE.
PRIVATE ROOM--MEMBERS ONLY.
I JUST JOINED.
SNOKT
KUHKRATCH
uhrrRRR

HUMANS ARE NOTHING BUT *MEAT* TO THINGS LIKE YOU--NO REASON TO *PICK* AND *CHOOSE*...

SO EMIL VARNER MUST HAVE *PAID* ONE OF YOU TO SINGLE OUT MY PARENTS AND THE FIVE OTHERS.
TO DO WHAT WE DO BEST.. AND ENJOY MOST.

THEN YOU *ADMIT* IT.
ARE *YOU* THE ONE I FACED BEFORE? THE ONE WHO ESCAPED WITH THE *DOORMAN'S HELP?*

HARD TO TELL, ISN'T IT? HARD TO SEE A SCAR THROUGH ALL THIS FUR...
AND TO HUMANS LIKE YOU, WE ALL LOOK ALIKE.
RUHRRRR

YOU'RE *RIGHT.*
TO ME, YOU'RE *ALL* SAVAGE KILLERS--NOTHING BUT *RABID BEASTS.*

SO I'LL JUST HAVE TO TAKE YOU *ALL DOWN*...
...AND LET THE *SILVER* SORT YOU OUT.

SHRRRP
SHRRET
RAIEEK

CHUFT
SHREDT

RAHR
CHTCH

NOW DIE.
AND CHANGE.

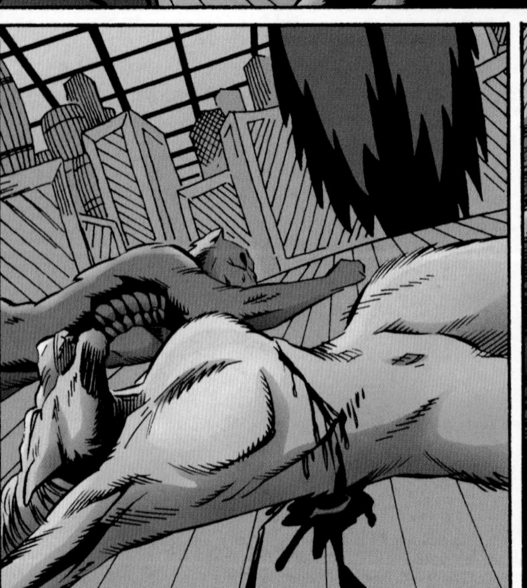

THE SCAR.
THIS ONE.
THE ASSASSIN.
MY PARENTS' MURDERER.
SH-KLK
FWOOM
BURNT OFFERING.

THE LOCATION OF THE POWER BEHIND YOUR ZOMBIE HAS BEEN SOURCED.
IF RAVENSWOOD IS WHAT YOU SEE THROUGH MY EYES...
Mnhn?
...THEN RAVENSWOOD IS WHAT YOU SHOULD SEEK THROUGH YOURS.
YOU HAVE MY THANKS, CAT MAJIK...
...BUT I'M STILL NOT IN THE MOOD.
IN THAT CASE, AS YOU SAY...
SOME OTHER TIME.
MRRAOW

STILLWATER CHURCH:
BE UNAFRAID, HOLY ONE...
WH-WHO--?
A FRIEND--AND FELLOW FOE OF DARKNESS.
YOURS IS THE ONLY REMAINING CHURCH IN GOTHAM--AND I NEED YOUR BLESSING.
ALTHOUGH YOUR OUTER ASPECT IS FEARSOME, MY SON, I SENSE GOODNESS WITHIN YOU.
WHATEVER YOU NEED, YOU SHALL HAVE.
CASTLE RAVENSWOOD: DESERTED FOR YEARS, YET TONIGHT EMITTING STRANGE LIGHT FROM ITS HIGH WINDOW...
NOW THAT THE BAT MAY KNOW THE PUNCHLINE, THIS PATCHWORK JOKE HAS RUN ITS COURSE.
TIME FOR A BETTER BODY--ONE BUILT FOR BEAUTY AND ANONYMITY RATHER THAN GARISH REVENGE...

AND NOW THAT I CAN REANIMATE ANY DEAD THING, ALL I NEED IS A FRESH CORPSE, SOMEONE WHO DIED YOUNG, INTO WHICH I CAN TRANSFER MY SOUL AND--
BRASH
ZZZT
IT'S OVER, VARNER!
THE MAJIK WOMAN'S EYES WERE TRUE...
...BUT THE SIGHT OF VARNER'S NEW FORM IS MORE GROTESQUE THAN I COULD HAVE IMAGINED.
UH OH.
YOUR TRUE BODY IS DEAD--AND YOU WILL STEAL NO MORE LIFE!
WORST OF ALL IS THE HIDEOUS DISTORTION OF MY OWN FATHER'S FACE.
DARK LORDS-- YOUR SERVANT CALLS ON YOU! HELP ME!!

HAH!

THE *TRUE* AGENTS OF EVIL--DARING TO *SHOW* YOURSELVES...

...MERE *SHADES* MADE *REAL.*

HEH HEH HEH-- I **KNEW** THEY WOULDN'T FAIL ME.

VARNER WAS *WEAKER* THAN THE OTHERS IN THE "INVISIBLE COLLEGE"--AND HE RESORTED TO *SORCERY,* ALLOWED YOU TO *POSSESS* HIM.

ALLOWED YOU TO *USE* HIM--HIM AND THE *WEREWOLF*...

...TO KILL MY PARENTS AND THE OTHER FIVE BECAUSE THEY WERE *NOT* WEAK--BECAUSE THEY HAD THE COURAGE AND THE WILL TO *OPPOSE YOUR EVIL!*
AND BECAUSE THEIR **SOULS,** FALSE BAT, ARE THEREFORE THE **SWEETEST.**

IF YOU CAN *CATCH* THEM.
WE HAVE FEASTED ON **THREE ALREADY,** WITH THE **FOURTH** SOUL JUST **CAPTURED.**
YOU **TELL** HIM, BOYS.

WHO *IS* THE FOURTH?
WHY SHOULD YOU **CARE** WHOSE ROTTING FLESH IT ONCE **INHABITED?** THE SOUL IS **OURS** NOW, IN THE **DOMAIN** YOU **CANNOT ENTER** ...SHORT OF **YOUR OWN** DEATH.
WHO--?

PERHAPS SYKES... PERHAPS RINCONI... OR JUST PERHAPS...
...YOUR MOTHER!

NYAHRRRR!

FADING--NOTHING TO GRASP, NOTHING TO CRUSH...
YOU CANNOT TOUCH US, BAT, NOT WHILE YOU ARE BOUND IN FLESH, NOT WHILE YOU ARE MORTAL.

THEN NOR CAN YOU TOUCH ME, HELL-SPAWN.
AH, BUT WE CAN... THROUGH THE HANDS OF OUR FLESH PUPPETS.
LIKE VARNER--WHOSE SCIENCE WAS ENHANCED BY YOUR SORCERY...

...ENABLING HIM TO CREATE AND INHABIT HIS FOUL PATCHWORK-JOKER BODY.
PRECISELY!
HYAH!

'EAR ME, EMONS!
I WILL NEVER BE STOPPED BY THE LIKES OF VARNER.
IT REMAINS TO BE SEEN...BUT OUR PUPPET HAS ALREADY SERVED US WELL, COMMANDING PUPPETS OF HIS OWN.
THE ZOMBIES.

VARNER RIPPED THEM FROM THEIR GRAVES AT YOUR BIDDING--TO DO NOTHING BUT KILL, AND RELEASE MORE SOULS FOR YOU TO HUNT.
OUR HUNGER IS HUGE.
EVER GROWING.
NEVER SATED.

AND I CAN'T STOP YOUR FEEDING--NOT YET, NOT TONIGHT...
SHKLK

NEVER.
FSHSHT
MAYBE NOT, BUT I CAN STOP THE KILLING...

...BY STOPPING YOUR PUPPETS--VARNER AND ANY FUTURE ZOMBIES!
FSHSHSHSH
WATER?

AS CAL WARNED, THE "ROAD" TO VARNER IS PAVED WITH DEMONS.
HWEH? YOU'RE LETTING HIM THROUGH? YOU'RE NOT PROTECTING ME?!
THE WATER, VARNER, HAS BEEN BLESSED.
BUT AS I VOWED, THIS ROAD IS MINE.
AND YOU FEAR IT?
YOU'RE AFRAID OF HOLY WATER?!
WE CHOOSE TO AVOID IT.
THEN YOU'RE ABANDONING ME?! LETTING ME FACE THIS... THIS BAT ON MY OWN?!
HE IS A MERE MAN--IN THE MASQUE OF BAT.
HAH!
SO I HAVE TO SERVE YOU--BUT YOU CAN JUST FORSAKE ME? IS THAT IT?!
DEALS WITH DEVILS, VARNER...
...NEVER PAY.
VERY WELL, THROW ME TO THE BAT! LEAVE ME TO MY OWN DEVICES! SEE IF I CARE!
SPRAKZZZ
I'LL STILL WIN!

I'LL BEAT THE BAT TO A SIZZLE--KILL HIM WITH THE SAME SPARKS THAT GAVE MY BODY LIFE!
FRAZZZ
YOU'VE GONE MAD, VARNER!
THE TRANSFER OF YOUR SOUL INTO THAT CORRUPT BODY HAS DRIVEN YOUR MIND INSANE.
OH, REALLY?
KZZZZZ
AS IF YOUR TRANSFORMATION, YOUNG WAYNE, IS NORMAL? AS IF YOU HAVEN'T GONE BATTY?
AND SO WHAT IF I'M MAD? I'M GOING TO LIVE FOREVER! THE PACKAGING MAY BE UGLY, BUT I GET TO KEEP MY SOUL--
--WHILE YOU'RE GOING TO DIE!
NOT TONIGHT, JOKER, AND NOT BEFORE YOU!
HAH! YOU'RE FIGHTING REFLEXES AS GOOD AS YOUR OWN! IN FACT, YOU INHERITED THEM!
WHICH IS WHY I'VE COME FOR YOUR HEAD, JOKER--THE HEAD YOU STOLE FROM MY FATHER!
POSSESSION IS NINE-TENTHS OF THE LAW, BATS--MAKING THIS SKULL-FACE MINE NOW!
HYEEHAHAHAAA

YOU THINK THAT'S FUNNY?
CHUFT
IF IT ISN'T, THEN SHOW ME HOW SERIOUS YOU ARE! COME ON--HIT ME!
PUNCH YOUR POOR DEAD DAD'S FACE!
HYAH!!
THRAKK
SHRASH
H-HE... HE D-DID IT?
S-STOP HIM, DARK LORDS... YOU'VE G-GOT TO HELP ME!
YOU N-NEED ME...TO KEEP KILLING...AND PROVIDING SOULS!
THEY COULDN'T CARE LESS ABOUT YOU, VARNER...

YOU'RE NOT WORTH A BLISTER TO THEM.
EVEN WHEN I WIN, THEY CAN'T LOSE, NOT REALLY...
HUH?

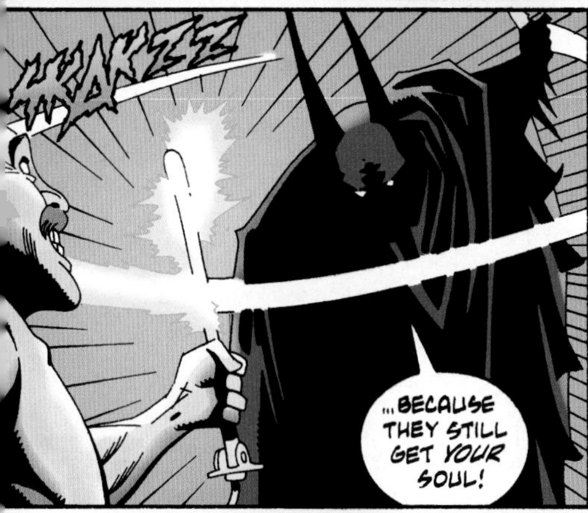
...BECAUSE THEY STILL GET YOUR SOUL!

AND MAY THEY CHEW IT TO SHREDS.
FROOSH

WHA--?
FIRST WATER--AND NOW FIRE?

YAOWTCH!
MY HAND--!

THE HAND, BODY-THIEF, IS NOT YOURS!

SHRUKT
NOR IS MY FATHER'S HEAD!
I'VE CUT YOUR PUPPET'S STRINGS, DARK ONES.
HIS SOUL IS GONE FROM THIS REALM-- AND LOOSE IN YOURS!
CHASE IT THROUGH THE MIST AND SHADOWS...
CATCH IT.
AND CHOKE ON IT.
DEFEATED AT THIS LEVEL, THEY FADE TO THE NEXT--AND I CAN ALMOST HEAR THE SHRIEKS OF EMIL VARNER'S FLEEING SOUL.

AND WHEN I HAVE RESTORED MY FATHER'S REMAINS, RESEALED HIS CASKET, REFILLED HIS GRAVE...
IT IS DONE, FATHER, AND MAY THIS SECOND BURIAL END YOUR SUFFERING.
MAY YOUR BODY NOW REST IN PEACE.
MY BODY MEANS NOTHING, BRUCE, AND VARNER'S ATROCITY WAS MERE AMUSEMENT TO THEM.
I KNOW, FATHER, BUT...
THEY'RE AFTER ME--THE SOUL OF ME--AND THEY'LL NEVER STOP HUNTING.
WE HURT THEM, BRUCE, THE SIX OF US IN THE INVISIBLE COLLEGE, AND YOUR MOTHER TOO.
WE KEPT THEM ALMOST IN CHECK, SET THEIR GOAL BACK, EVEN TOOK A FEW OF THEM DOWN, BELIEVE IT OR NOT...
AND OF US ALL, BRUCE, I HURT THEM MOST.

THEY WANT REVENGE.
MY SOUL WILL BE AMONG THE SWEETEST THE DARK LORDS HAVE EVER TASTED...
AND YOUR MOTHER... BY ALL THAT'S GOOD AND HOLY, BRUCE... YOU MUST HELP HER!
WHERE... WHERE IS SHE, FATHER?
I... I DON'T KNOW! SHE WON'T APPEAR TO ME...!
I'VE LOOKED, BRUCE, AND I'M LOOKING STILL, SEARCHING EVERYWHERE--BUT I CAN'T FIND HER! WE CAN ONLY PRAY SHE'S MERELY HIDING, BUT I FEAR SHE MAY BE LOST!
MAYBE CAPTIVE, BRUCE! THEY COULD BE TORMENTING AND PERVERTING HER GOODNESS EVEN NOW!
THEY CAN'T DEVOUR A NOBLE SOUL, YOU SEE--THEY HAVE TO RUIN IT BEFORE THEY CAN FEAST!
AND IF THE SOUL IS PURE ENOUGH, IT COULD TAKE YEARS OF--
STOP IT, FATHER!
YEARS OF UNENDING AGONY, BRUCE, BEFORE THEY CRIPPLE AND DARKEN HER ENOUGH TO END IT!
AND THE WAY THEY'LL END IT--BY CONSUMING HER, AND MAKING HER PART OF THEM! IT'S TOO HIDEOUS TO--
FATHER--ENOUGH!

HOW DO WE FIND HER?!
I DON'T KNOW, SON, BUT YOU CAN'T STOP! IT'S NOT OVER!
EVEN IF THEY DON'T HAVE HER, THEY'RE HUNTING--
--JUST AS THEY'RE HUNTING ME, CLOSING IN RIGHT NOW!
I BECOME VULNERABLE EVERY TIME I MANIFEST-- RISKING MY SOUL JUST TO SEE YOU--
YOU HEAR ME, BRUCE? THEY'RE EVERYWHERE IN THIS DAMNED CITY!
I CAN'T STAY-- AND YOU CAN'T STOP!
YOU'VE BEGUN A WAR YOU MUST FIGHT TO THE FINISH!
AS LONG AS GOTHAM REMAINS HAUNTED...
...YOU CAN NEVER STOP!
NEVER, FATHER...

...EVEN IF I AM FOREVER HAUNTED...

...AND FOREVER HUNTED...

...BY ALL THE HORRORS OF HELL.

KELLEY JONES
JOHN BEATTY

ANOTHER INVASION FROM THE UNDERWORLD--THE THIRD OUTBREAK THIS WEEK, EACH RAVAGING A DIFFERENT AREA OF HAUNTED GOTHAM...
THEY'RE STILL GATHERING, GORDON! WAIT FOR ALL OF THEM!
IT'S NOT EASY, BUT WE'RE HOLDING!
HAUNTED GOTHAM—PART THREE
THE SHATTERED SERPENT

IN ALL THREE INVASIONS, THE SNAKES HAVE BEEN ENTIRELY PHYSICAL CREATURES...
YAAH!
WHA--?!
...WITH ONLY THE SUDDENNESS OF THEIR APPEARANCE HINTING AT ANYTHING SUPERNATURAL.
WHAT THE--?!
HSSSS
THE PHENOMENON IS BIZARRE.
UNCANNY.
TERRIFYING.
BUT THE SERPENTS THEMSELVES ARE UTTERLY NORMAL, THEIR HORROR DERIVING SOLELY FROM CIRCUMSTANCE.
THEY DO NOT BELONG IN THE CITY-- AND CERTAINLY NOT IN SUCH IMPOSSIBLE ABUNDANCE.
COMMISSIONER GORDON, HOW MUCH LONGER BEFORE--
JUST HOLD YOUR BOMB, OFFICER KNIGHT!

THE FIRST INVASION ENDED IN A MESSY CHAOS OF BLOOD-SLICKED STREETS.
NOW!
THE SECOND ONSLAUGHT WAS STILL HARROWING, BUT GORDON AND I HAD LEARNED NOT TO SQUASH OR SLASH THE THINGS.
BWOOFFFF
TONIGHT WE'RE FULLY PREPARED AND THIS ATTACK SHOULD BE ROUTINE IF--
KLUMP
Unh!
MY NOSE-FILTER!
HRAAHHHHH
GOT TO HOLD MY BREATH--KEEP THE GAS OUT OF MY OWN LUNGS.
TO THE BAT! PULL THAT THING OFF HIM!
PYTHON'S HELPING--CONSTRICTING MY CHEST--PREVENTING ME FROM INHALING.
OT TO HOLD OUT LONGER THAN THE ERPENT-- GET FREE AND REACH MY REATHER BEFORE PASSING OUT...
IT'S TOO STRONG, SIR!
PULL HARDER, KNIGHT!

PYTHON'S SUCCUMBING, EASING ITS DEATH-GRIP...
IF NOT FOR THE GAS, I COULD ACTUALLY BREATHE--BUT STILL CAN'T REACH MY FILTER...
VISION DIMMING--ABOUT TO LOSE IT...
LET GO, DAMMIT!
ONE LAST CHANCE... GOT TO--
SWUNT
--ADD SOME PUNCH TO THE GAS.
DID IT... BUT TOO LATE... TOO WEAK...
CAN'T REACH THE FILTER...
CAN'T...
BREATHE--NOW!
Shhhh
THANKS, GORDON. LET'S SWEEP THE HOUSES FOR ANY REMAINING SNAKES.
RIGHT--AND FOR CLUES WE COULDN'T FIND THE FIRST TWO TIMES...

OME HINT OF ERE THIS AGUE IS MING OM."
YES, ANCIENT ONE, I SHALL CONVEY YOUR NEEDS TO THE OPHILIATORS AT ONCE...
...FOR THE FLESH AND THE BLOOD IS DEATH AND LIFE EVERLASTING.
P-PLEASE...LET US OUT!
SILENCE! YOURS IS THE FLESH FROM WHICH LIFE EVERLASTING WILL BE CONSUMED!
WE RE YOURS, ANCIENT ONES!
FILL OUR MINDS WITH THE FORCE OF YOUR WILL!
SPEAK TO US THROUGH LORD OPHIDIAN!
I HAVE JUST SPOKEN TO THE ANCIENT ONE HERE ON EARTH--
--SENT DOWN TO US ACROSS VAST GULFS OF TIME AND SPACE.
AND WHAT IS HIS COMMAND, LORD OPHIDIAN?

HIS WILL IS THE SAME-- THIS WORLD OVERWHELMED BY CHAOS AND DOOM!
SHIKA SHIKA SHIKA SHIKA
TO THAT END, THE ANCIENT ONES REQUIRE MORE FLESH AND BLOOD...

GO-- NOW!
AS THE ANCIENT ONE COMMANDS, LORD OPHIDIAN, SO SHALL WE OBEY!

NO CLUES AGAIN, AND THE WHOLE THING STILL MAKES NO SENSE...

THERE MUST BE AN INTELLIGENCE BEHIND THIS-- SOME HUMAN AGENCY...
OR SOME DEMONIC AGENCY, COMMIS-SIONER.
BUT WHO, OFFICER KNIGHT? WHERE DO THE SNAKES COME FROM?

THE ANSWER TO THAT MAY SOLVE OUR OTHER ONGOING MYSTERY.
YOU MEAN ALL THE MISSING PERSONS?
SOME OF THE SNAKES ARE VENOMOUS, COMMISSIONER GORDON-- AND A SMALL PROPORTION COULD EVEN KILL HUMANS.
BUT NO PLAGUE OF SERPENTS, NOT EVEN A BIBLICAL ONE, COULD MAKE SO MANY BODIES DISAPPEAR...

"SO WHAT'S HAPPENING TO THEM?
"ARE THEY DEAD OR STILL ALIVE?
"HOW AND WHY DO THEY DISAPPEAR SO COMPLETELY?
"WHO'S TAKING THEM?
"WHERE ARE THEY?"
TRACK 29
WE RETURN, LORD OPHIDIAN, WITH THE FLESH AND THE BLOOD WHICH IS LIFE EVERLASTING.
YOU HAVE DONE WELL, OPHIOLATORS.
THE ANCIENT ONES ARE PLEASED...

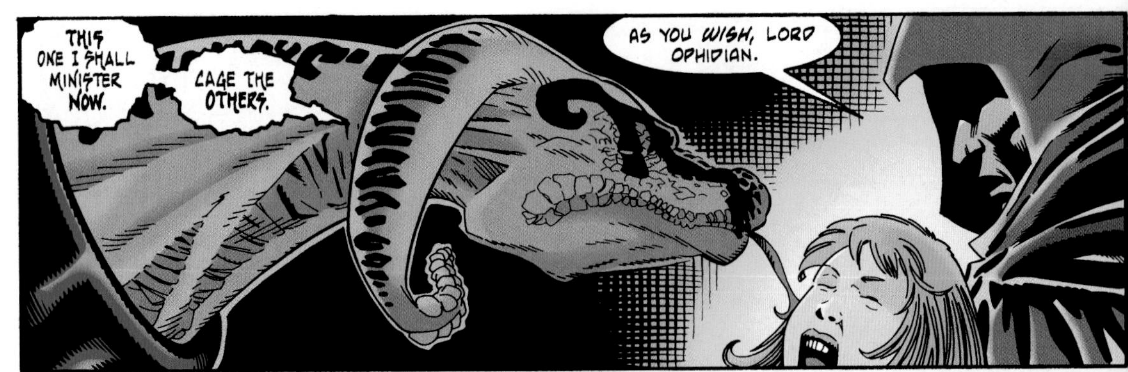

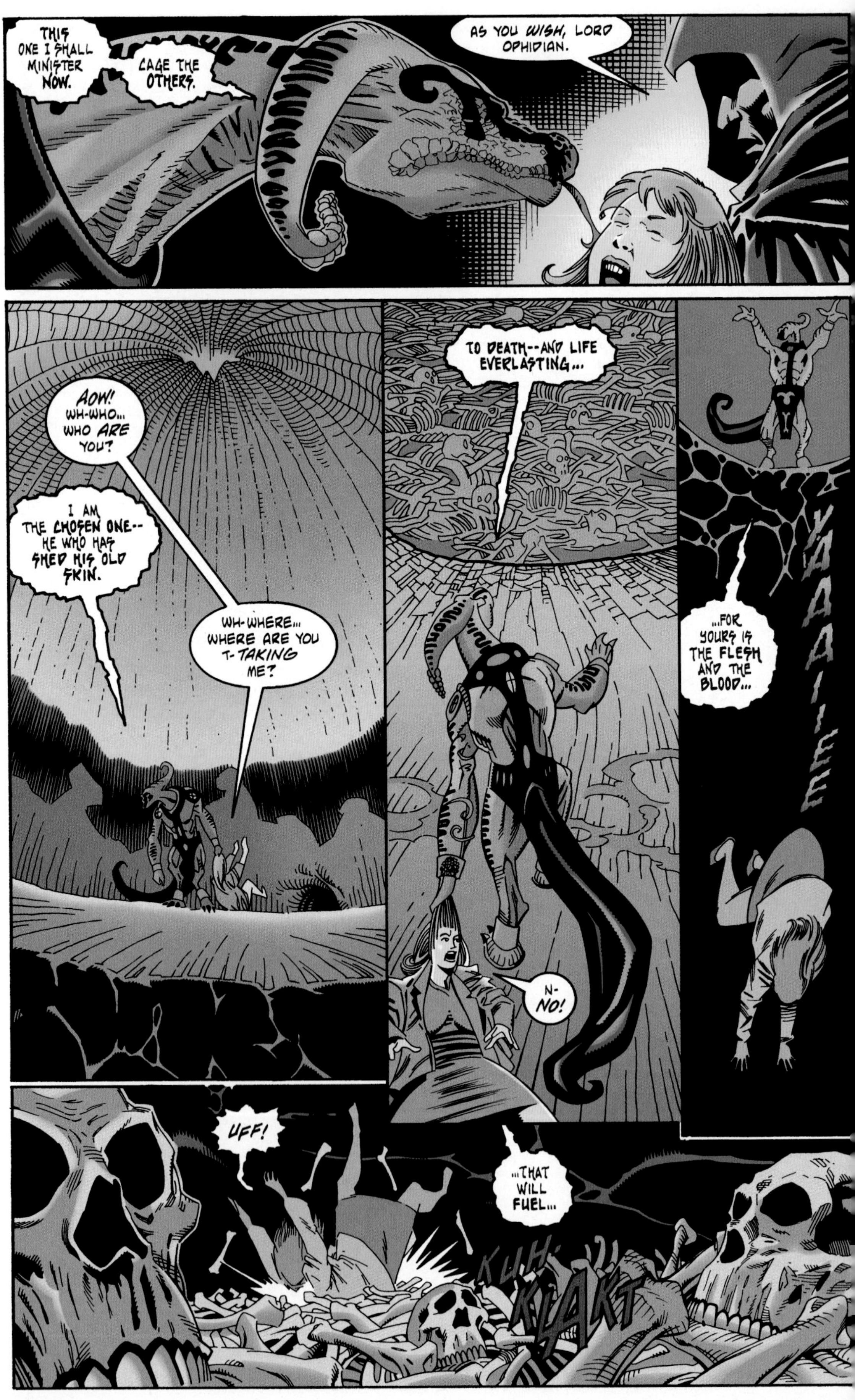

AOW! WH-WHO... WHO ARE YOU?

I AM THE CHOSEN ONE-- HE WHO HAS SHED HIS OLD SKIN.

WH-WHERE... WHERE ARE YOU T-TAKING ME?

TO DEATH--AND LIFE EVERLASTING...

N-NO!

...FOR YOURS IS THE FLESH AND THE BLOOD...

UFF!

...THAT WILL FUEL...

KUH-KLAKT

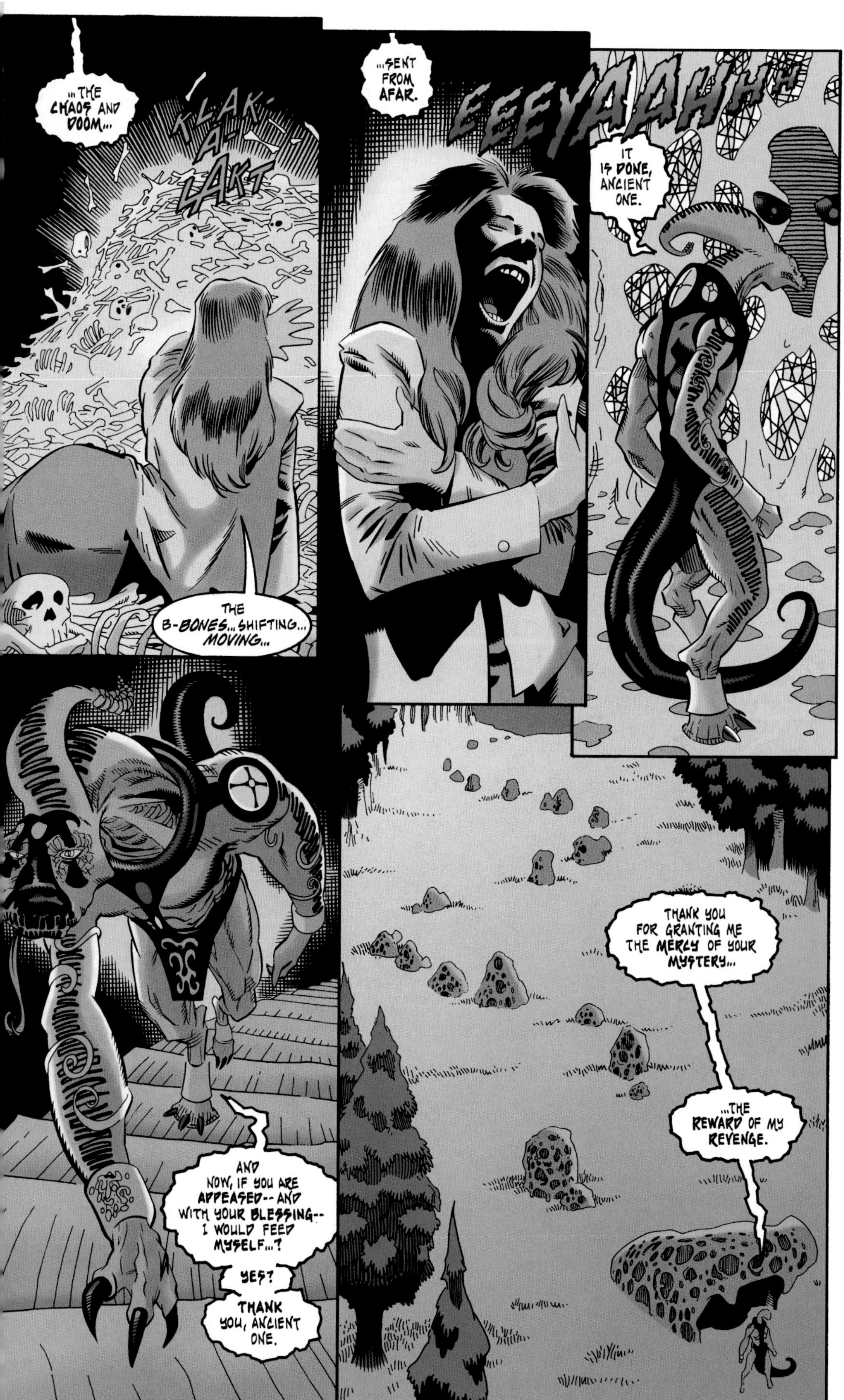
...THE CHAOS AND DOOM...
KLAK-A-LAKT
THE B-BONES... SHIFTING... MOVING...
...SENT FROM AFAR.
EEEYAAAHHH
IT IS DONE, ANCIENT ONE.
AND NOW, IF YOU ARE APPEASED-- AND WITH YOUR BLESSING-- I WOULD FEED MYSELF...?
YES?
THANK YOU, ANCIENT ONE.
THANK YOU FOR GRANTING ME THE MERCY OF YOUR MYSTERY...
...THE REWARD OF MY REVENGE.

MASTER BRUCE?
ARE YOU DOWN THERE, SIR?
WHAT IS IT?
YES, ALFRED!
COMMISSIONER GORDON'S SIGNAL, SIR-- BUT NOT FROM POLICE HEADQUARTERS...
THEN WHERE?

THE LIGHT SEEMS TO BE RISING, SIR--

"--FROM THE LIMEKILL AREA."
WHERE THE DEVIL IS HE? LOUSY SIGNAL'S BEEN SHINING FOR TEN--
GPD

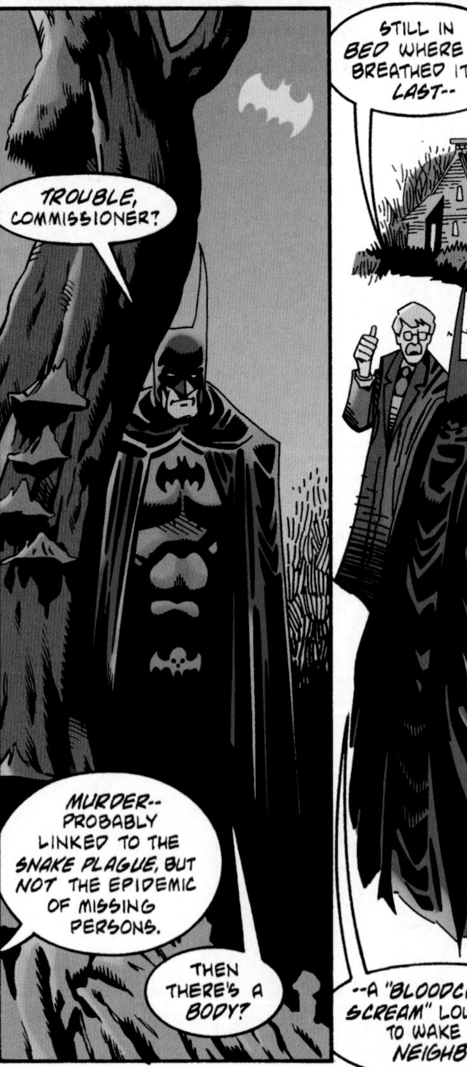
TROUBLE, COMMISSIONER?
MURDER-- PROBABLY LINKED TO THE SNAKE PLAGUE, BUT NOT THE EPIDEMIC OF MISSING PERSONS.
THEN THERE'S A BODY?
STILL IN BED WHERE IT BREATHED ITS LAST--
--A "BLOODCURDLIN SCREAM" LOUD ENOU TO WAKE THE NEIGHBORS.

AND YOUR
ALL FOR HELP
MEANS YOU'RE
NOW WILLING
TO TRUST
ME?
YOU DID WELL WITH VARNER
AND THE WEREWOLVES, AND YOU'VE
BEEN A HELP WITH THE SNAKES...
BUT I STILL--
SHOW
ME THE BODY,
GORDON.
FANG PUNCTURES--
BUT IF IT WAS A
SNAKE, THE SPACING
SUGGESTS HUMAN
SIZE...
CASSANDRA
KNIGHT SUSPECTED
A VAMPIRE, BUT
THE VICTIM'S STILL
LIVID--LITTLE OR
NO BLOOD
STOLEN.
AND IT HAS A STRANGE COLOR
AND CONSISTENCY...
...AS
IF IT'S BEEN
THINNED.
DILUTED BY THE
INJECTION OF SOME KIND
OF VENOM LIKE THE
FIRST VICTIM.
THERE
WAS ONE BEFORE
THIS?
TWO
NIGHTS
AGO--
TILL IN THE MORGUE WITH
RONER GUNT."
IT'S NO
VENOM I CAN
IDENTIFY...
PLUS, IT SEEMS TO CONTAIN
REPTILIAN OVA.
EGGS?
MIXED IN
VENOM?
YEP--FROM
AN UNKNOWN SNAKE
GENUS.
IN
FACT, THE DNA
SEEMS UTTERLY
ALIEN.

THE SHEET-- IT'S MOVING!
WHA--?!
STAY BACK--BOTH OF YOU!
SNAKES, ALL RIGHT-- INCUBATED INSIDE THE BODY...
CONTAINERS, GUNT!
I'LL COLLECT THEM-- AND YOU'LL IDENTIFY THEM.
SPECIMEN JARS OR--
ANYTHING BEFORE THE WRIGGLE FREE!
Botched Demon Summoning
SACRIFICED POLITICIAN
HOMICIDAL HOMUNCULUS
MEANWHILE:
YOU HAVE TRAVELED THE COLD VOID, ANCIENT ONE, CHOOSING ME AS YOUR SERVANT ON EARTH...
...ENTRUSTING ME TO PROVIDE THE FLESH AND THE BLOOD TO FEED CHAOS AND-- WHAT? YES... YOU'RE RIGHT.
YOUR WILL MUST BE FURTHER AMPLIFIED-- THROUGH AN EARTHLY FOCUS FOR THE ENERGY FROM OPHIUCHUS.
IN MISTHAVEN.
I SHALL ATTEND TO IT AT ONCE, ANCIENT ONE.
THE NEXT NIGHT AT, POLICE H.Q.:
THIS IS A SURVEILLANCE TAPE FROM A JEWELRY STORE IN THE MISTHAVEN AREA.

ANOTHER GEMSTONE BURGLARY, COMMISSIONER, BUT WHAT DOES THIS HAVE TO DO WITH--
JUST WAIT...

THERE! YOU SEE? A REPTILIAN HUMANOID...

AND YOU THINK IT'S THE EGG-VENOM KILLER?
IT'S YOUR "HUMAN-SIZE SNAKE," ISN'T IT?
GRANTED...

BUT WHY WOULD A SNAKE-MAN WANT TO STEAL GEMS?
I WAS HOPING YOU'D HAVE A CLUE.
NOT YET.
ANY LINKS BETWEEN THE TWO MURDER VICTIMS?
BOTH WERE THE SAME AGE AND ONCE LIVED NEAR EACH OTHER...
MAYBE ONE. BUT IT'S A STRETCH.

KNIGHT CROSS-CHECKED LL OTHER MISSING PERSONS OF THAT AGE.
SHE FOUND NINE WHO ONCE LIVED IN THE SAME NEIGHBORHOOD AND TTENDED THE SAME HIGH SCHOOL.
MAYBE NOT SUCH A STRETCH...

YES?
NO PROGRESS FROM CORONER GUNT, SIR-- SAYS THE SNAKE HATCHLINGS MAY BE IMPOSSIBLE TO IDENTIFY.
ALL RIGHT, KEEP ME UPDATED.
ONE OTHER THING, COMMISSIONER...

SILENT ALARM ACTIVATED AT THE MUSEUM--TWO UNITS RESPONDING NOW.
HOLD THEM BACK, GORDON! I'LL HANDLE IT!
WHAT? WHY?
BECAUSE THE MUSEUM JUST OPENED A TRAVELING EXHIBIT OF PRECIOUS STONES.
IT'S THE REPTOID--
"--AND HE'S AFTER SOME-THING."
HALL of MINERALS
PRECIOUS GEMS
MORE CRYSTALS, ANCIENT ONES, ATTUNED TO THE VIBRATIONS OF YOUR ENERGY...
DONATED BY MARSHALL AUSTIN
SPECIAL EXHIBIT OF RARE GEMS
...THEIR FACETS AMPLIFYING THE STARLIGHT OF YOUR CONSTELLATION...
...FOCUSING THE WILL OF THE SERPENT BEARER INTO THE MINDS OF YOUR CHOSEN FOLLOWERS.
IT IS HIM.
THE SAME HUMANOID SERPENT CAPTURED BY THE SURVEILLANCE CAMERA-- A THIEF AS WELL AS A MURDERER-- BUT WHY NOT STEAL CASH? WHY FOCUS ON GEMS?

--? DANGER, ANCIENT ONE?
ZHEMM
ABOVE--?
BLINDING LIGHT...
...HITTING THE GLASS!
SKYLIGHT MELTING--GIVING WAY!
WUMP
OPHILIATORS--TAKE HIM!
TRANSPORT HIS FLESH AND BLOOD THROUGH THE TUNNELS--FOR SACRIFICE TO CHAOS!

CLOSING ON ME... GOT TO--
SH-KLIK
FROOOM
--BUY SOME SPACE.
STAND FAST! PROTECT LORD OPHIDIAN!
HWWUKK
THE REPTOID--
GETTING AWAY WITH HIS LOOT.
THRAKK
CAN'T PURSUE-- UNTIL I GET PAST HIS FOLLOWERS.

LAST ONE.
SNOK
GROUND FLOOR, YET HE WENT DOWN-- AS IF AWARE THAT THE POLICE HAVE THE MUSEUM SURROUNDED.
EVEN SO, HIDING IN THE BASEMENT WON'T HELP HIM FOR LONG--UNLESS HE'S NOT HIDING AT ALL--
...BUT ESCAPING--LIKE A REAL SERPENT THROUGH A FRESHLY BURROWED TUNNEL.
THE SILENT ALARM WAS TRIPPED INTERNALLY-- AT THE GEM EXHIBIT--NOT BY A BREAK-IN THROUGH ONE OF THE DOORS.
EY HAD ACCESS OM THE SEWER STEM--AND IT'S LABYRINTH TTING THE TIRE CITY.
BY NOW, HE COULD BE ANYWHERE IN THE MAZE.

GOTHAM MUSEUM of NATURAL HISTORY
THE SNAKE-MAN GOT AWAY, GORDON, BUT THERE ARE OTHERS IN HERE.
GOTHAM POLICE

HE HAD ACCOMPLICES?
MORE LIKE FOLLOWERS OR CULTISTS-- AND THEY CALLED HIM "LORD OPHIDIAN."
HOW MANY?

SIX, AND YOUR PEOPLE CAN TAKE FIVE INTO CUSTODY.
I NEED ONE...

"...FOR INTERROGATION."
Catherine Majik
seer*astrologer*tarot
palmist*scryer*oracle
crystal-gazer*medium*exorcist
kabbalist*numerologist
wiccan
occultist*voudun priestess
YOU HELPED ME ONCE, CAT MAJIK...

AND THIS TIME I'LL HAVE MORE THAN A MERE ZOMBIE-FINGER TO WORK WITH-- AN ENTIRE BODY, NO LESS.
A MIND-CONTROLLED SNAKE CULTIST. CAN YOU MAKE HIM TALK?
WHAT WILL YOU GIVE ME?

GRATITUDE-- FOR HELPING ME SAVE LIVES.

AND
REVENTING AN
CREASE IN THE
PULATION OF
RESTLESS
GHOSTS.
DO YOU
KNOW THE
XPRESSION,
YOU WISH TO
ST IN PEACE,
IE NOT IN
GOTHAM"?
YES.
WISE
WORDS...
SINCE THE
DARK LORDS
HAUNTING
GOTHAM
REALLY HAVE
BLOCKED
THE WAY TO
HEAVEN.
MAKING
LIFE IN THE
CITY ALL
THE MORE
PRECIOUS.
AND
DEATH ALL THE MORE
TERRIFYING.
WATCH THE CRYSTAL.
THE CULTIST
WILL SPEAK THROUGH
ME--AS HIS MENTAL IMAGES
ARE CAPTURED BETWEEN
MY HANDS.
QUICKLY, CAT
MAJIK.
BE PATIENT
UNTIL I HAVE
ATTAINED
RANCE-UNION
WITH--
IT BEGAN AT THE END,
WITH DEATH PLOTTED FROM
THE BEGINNING...
...WHEN
STRANGE STONE
WAS SENT FORTH FROM
THE SERPENT BEARER
CONSTELLATION OF
OPHIUCHUS.

THE METEOR BROKE UP AND SLAMMED THE EARTH IN AN ELONGATED PATTERN OF DIABASE ROCK.. THE "SERPENTINE" STONE CALLED OPHITE...
...THUS FORMING, ON THE OUTSKIRTS OF GOTHAM, A "SHATTERED SNAKE."
FROM AN ELECTRICAL STORM CAUSED BY VIOLATION OF THE ATMOSPHERE, FORKED TONGUES OF LIGHTNING LICKED THE ALIEN STONES UNTIL THEY GLOWED.
AND WHEN THE RAINS LASHED DOWN ON THE CHARRED AND HEATED BOULDERS, THE SHATTERED SNAKE SIZZLED.
HSSSSS
"AS THE STONES COOLED, THEY RANG WITH THE VIBRATIONS OF HAMMERED CRYSTAL...
"...THE SCREAM OF A SEVERED SNAKE."
THEREAFTER, BECAUSE NO WILDLIFE WOULD APPROACH THE BOULDERS... AND NO BIRDS OR INSECTS WOULD FLY ABOVE THEM...
YES--?

CONTINUE, CAT MAJIK.
IT WAS SUSPECTED THAT THE ALIEN SERPENT EMANATED A CONSTANT SUB-AUDIBLE TRILLING... EVER SILENT BUT ALWAYS SPEAKING TO THOSE WHO COULD HEAR BEYOND SOUND.
WHO?
ENTER JEREMY ADDER--
--WHOSE VERY NAME SUGGESTS A PREORDAINED DESTINY AS SERVANT OF THE ANCIENT SERPENT BEARERS.
"ONE NIGHT, AS IF LURED BY INVISIBLE SIRENS OR SOME PHANTOM PIPER, YOUNG JEREMY LEFT HIS BED IF NOT HIS SLUMBER...
"AFTER SLEEPWALKING TO THE OUTSKIRTS OF GOTHAM, HE GOT DOWN ON HIS BELLY AND WRIGGLED INTO THE OPHITE EMISSARY'S MOUTH, LULLED AND TRANSFIXED FOR HOURS BY THE SINGING STONE.
"HE SLITHERED FREE JUST BEFORE DAWN, SLEEPWALKING BACK TO HIS BED... BUT ONLY TO REPEAT HIS NIGHTLY INDOCTRINATIONS FOR YEARS."

DURING THIS PERIOD JEREMY ADDER BECAME OBSESSED WITH THREE SUBJECTS--ASTRONOMY, AT LEAST INSOFAR AS IT INVOLVED GAZING AT OPHIUCHUS FOR HOURS ON END...
GEOLOGY--BUT CONFINED TO THE STUDY OF OPHITE AND CRYSTALS...
AND HERPETOLOGY, THE STUDY OF SNAKES--WITH ITS OFFSHOOT, OPHIOLATRY, THE WORSHIP OF SNAKES.
INDEED, HE IMMERSED HIMSELF IN THE LORE OF WORLDWIDE SNAKE CULTS.
"THE FIRST PHYSICAL CHANGE OCCURRED IN HIS MID-TEENS, WHEN JEREMY DEVELOPED THE EXTREMELY RARE CONDITION OF POIKILOTHERMISM.
"LIKE A REPTILE, HIS BODY ASSUMED THE TEMPERATURE OF ITS ENVIRONMENT--AND NOW THAT HE WAS COLD-BLOODED, HIS NOCTURNAL VISITS TO THE SHATTERED SNAKE BECAME VITAL.
"THE STONE OF HIS OPHITE WOMB, YOU SEE, WAS WARM--GIVING OFF CONSTANT HEAT, AS WELL AS ANOTHER FORM OF RADIATION...

IT CAUSED MUTATION.
EVEN AS JEREMY ADDER'S SKIN TURNED SCALY, HIS TONGUE LENGTHENED AND SPLIT...
"HIS PUPILS BECAME VERTICAL SLITS BEHIND NICTITATING MEMBRANES.
"HIS HAIR FELL OUT AND HIS TEETH GREW TO SHARP FANGS WHICH WERE FOUND TO BE HOLLOW."
ULTRASOUND SCANS REVEALED ANOMALOUS GLANDS ABOVE THE FANGS-- WHICH, WHEN MILKED, SECRETED A FLUID RESEMBLING VENOM.
MOST UNUSUAL.
skwt
"BY THE TIME JEREMY HAD BEEN MIRACULOUSLY RESHAPED IN THE IMAGE OF HIS SERPENT BEARER CREATORS, HIS DOCTOR COULD ONLY DIAGNOSE--
SOME MYSTERIOUS TRANSFORMATIVE DISEASE OF THE BLOOD!
"HE WAS SWIFTLY OSTRACIZED...
"...SCORNED AND RIDICULED BY HIS CLASSMATES."
HEY, SNAKEFACE!
NICE FANGS, FREAK!

AND SOME OF THE CLASSMATES LATER BECAME HIS VICTIMS-- THEIR DEAD BODIES INCUBATING THE HATCHLINGS.
"ONE NIGHT, ROUSED FROM A STUPOR BY HIS SON'S PETS, JEREMY'S FATHER SNAPPED.
H-HUH? WHA...? THAT DOES IT!
BEER
EARTH IN THE BALANCE
"HE FOUND JEREMY FEEDING...
YOU FREAK! YOU'RE NO SON OF MINE!
YOU'RE THE DEVIL'S SPAWN!
"AND WHEN JEREMY'S MOTHER TRIED TO INTERVENE...
NO! DON'T HURT OUR S--
BAOWM
BUT HOW DID HE BECOME "LORD OPHIDIAN"?
THROUGH TRAGEDY AND HORROR.
HIS HUMAN FATHER BECAME A DRUNK, WHILE HIS HUMAN MOTHER WEPT AND PRAYED TO A GOD WHO NEVER ANSWERED.
"...THE FATHER DOOMED HIMSELF.. TO BECOME OPHIDIAN'S FIRST HUMAN SACRAMENT."
FATHER, YOU HAVE NOT FED ME TONIGHT...YET.
YAAAHHH

OPHIDIAN KISSED MOTHER GOODBYE, INJECTING AS WELL--AND WHEN THE TWO IES HAD PROVIDED SUFFICIENT *INCUBATION*...
...HE LEFT THE HOME OF HIS FALSE PARENTS FOR THE *LAST TIME*...
...NOW ACCOMPANIED BY HIS *OWN* CHILDREN.
OPHIDIAN AND HIS OFFSPRING WENT STRAIGHT TO THE WARM BURROW OF THE SHATTERED SERPENT'S MOUTH--WHERE THEY MINGLED IN A WRITHING MASS FOR THREE DAYS AND THREE NIGHTS.
"AND THEN, WHETHER BY THE ACCIDENT OF WEIGHT AND GRAVITY OR THE DESIGN OF DISTANT STARS...
"...THEY COLLAPSED INTO A CAVERN ILLUMINATED BY THE GLOWING BOULDERS EMBEDDED IN ITS CEILING.
VE METEORITE HAD SO CAVED IN...
"...AND IT WAS THIS FRAGMENT OF ALIEN OPHITE--THIS SEGMENT OF THE SHATTERED SNAKE--WHICH BECAME THE *HEART* OF LORD OPHIDIAN'S *NEW HOME*."
YES, ANCIENT ONES... I SHALL OBEY.

IT ALSO BECAME THE FOCUS OF THE ANCIENT ONE'S WILL, CHANNELED OUTWARD BY LORD OPHIDIAN--TO GATHER US, HIS FAITHFUL OPHILIATORS.
WE EXTENDED THE CAVERN, DIGGING SERPENTINE TUNNELS UNDER EVERY REGION OF GOTHAM, THROUGH WHICH WE OBTAIN THE FLESH AND THE BLOOD OF SACRAMENTS FOR--
ENOUGH, CAT MAJIK!
BREAK YOUR TRANCE--AND TELL ME...
DO YOU BELIEVE WHAT YOU'VE JUST SAID?
WHAT THE OPHILIATOR SAID, BAT-MAN, THROUGH ME...
...AND IT WAS TRUTH--ACQUIRED THROUGH HIS MENTAL LINK WITH "OPHIDIAN" HIMSELF.
TRUTH THAT SOME INTELLIGENCE IN THE OPHIUCHUS CONSTELLATION DELIBERATELY SENT A METEOR TO CREATE THE "SHATTERED SNAKE"?
I SAY IT'S MADNESS.
SINGLED OUT JEREMY ADDER TO BE AFFECTED BY IT?
WHO CAN SAY?
AND SOME WOULD SAY THAT BELIEF IN "DEMONS" IS MADNESS--YET YOU HAVE PERSONALLY ENCOUNTERED THE DARK LORDS HOLDING GOTHAM IN THRALL.

BUT... ENTITIES FROM ANOTHER STAR SYSTEM ?
ELDRITCH TRADITION STATES THAT THE DARK LORDS ARE NOT NATIVE TO OUR REALMS OF LIFE OR DEATH...
...THAT INSTEAD THEY CAME TO THIS EARTH, ACROSS VAST GULFS OF TIME AND SPACE...
...TO EXIST HERE AS SOUL-PARASITES.
INDEED, OUR MYTHS OF DEMONS AND HELL MAY HAVE BEEN SHAPED BY DISTORTED PERCEPTIONS OF THESE OTHERWORLDLY PREDATORS.
FROM OPHIUCHUS--?
IS SATAN... NOT A SNAKE?
POINT TAKEN, BUT--
YOU ARE DOOMED... TO MATE WITH LORD OPHIDIAN... YOUR FLESH AND BLOOD FILLED WITH HIS SPAWN... EVEN AS HE FEASTS.
WHAT...?
GET HIM OUT OF HERE, BAT-MAN.
REMOVE THE OPHIOLATOR FROM MY PARLOR AND ENTER THE MOUTH OF HIS SHATTERED SNAKE-LORD AT YOUR OWN PERIL.
IT IS ME, MISTER AND MISTRESS WAYNE... YOUR SERVANT ALFRED PENNYWORTH, STILL FAITHFUL EVEN AFTER YOUR PASSING.
I CAN REPORT THAT YOUR SON HAS ACCEPTED HIS DESTINY AS THE BAT... BUT PERHAPS TOO FEARLESSLY, TOO RECKLESSLY.
I KNOW WE HAVE PREPARED HIM WELL, BUT I WORRY THAT HIS OPPOSITION IS--
THOOM THOOM THOOM
EH--?
KRUMPH

THE CAVERN WALL-- BREACHED!
BUT WHO--?
WE HAVE ERRED.
THIS IS NOT THE SOUTHERN SUBWAY ANNEX...
...NOT OUR GOAL.
BUT HE IS FLESH AND BLOOD...
TAKE HIM!
THE ELONGATED METEOR FIELD AT THE OUTSKIRTS OF GOTHAM--AND IT DOES RESEMBLE A BROKEN SNAKE, BUT I STILL CAN'T BELIEVE--
IT IS TRUE.
FATHER!
BUT... ALL THE WAY FROM OPHIUCHUS?
THE TIME REQUIRED TO CROSS THAT MUCH SPACE...
IN THIS REALM TO WHICH DEATH HAS CONSIGNED ME--RULED BY THE DARK LORDS--THERE IS NO TIME, NO SPACE.
THERE IS ONLY WILL, AND IF THE WILL IS STRONG ENOUGH AND DARK ENOUGH...
...ETERNITY ITSELF MELTS TO A MERE MOMENT.
YOU MUST BE STRONGER, MY SON, AND WASTE NOT A MOMENT MORE...

ENTER THE SNAKE--NOW--AND SLAY ITS HEART!
MY PRECISE INTENT, FATHER.
"AND THANKS TO CAT MAJIK, THE INSIDE OF THE SNAKE IS A MYSTERY ALREADY SOLVED...
klakt
"...ITS HEART AS GOOD AS DEAD."
NOT FROM THE SUBWAY, I'M TOLD, BUT STILL FIT TO FEED CHAOS--FOR YOURS IS THE FLESH AND THE BLOOD OF DEATH AND LIFE EVERLASTING...
SHIKKA SHIKKA
AND YOURS IS THE OFFAL OF HELL, MONSTER...
...THE SAME HELL AWAITING YOUR SOUL.
SILENCE!
SWAK
YOU DOUBT THAT YOUR BLOOD CAN BE SPLASHED--YOUR BONES STRIPPED?!

FAR FROM IT, MONSTER.
I AM WELL AWARE THAT DEATH STALKS US ALL--EVEN YOU.
YET YOU SMILE AT YOUR IMMINENT FATE?
NO...
KLUDT
AT YOURS.
SHRRRPP
HRHHHH
STAY BACK, ALFRED!
BUT HIS FANGS, SIR! IF HE'S THE MURDERER, THEY MUST BE VENOMOUS!

CHAKT
THEY'RE FATAL...

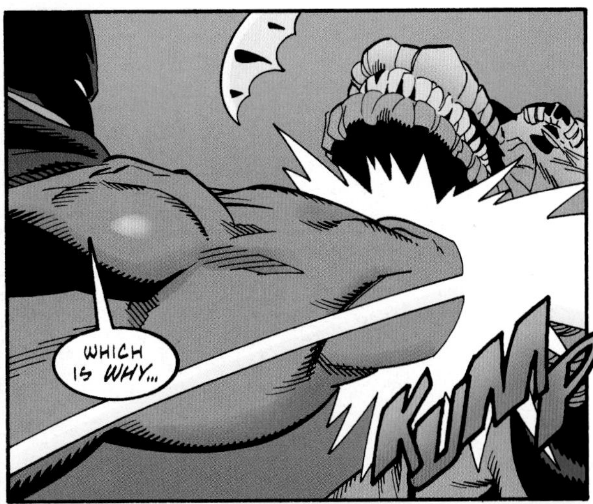
WHICH IS WHY...
KUMP

CHUFT
...I'M COMMANDING YOU...

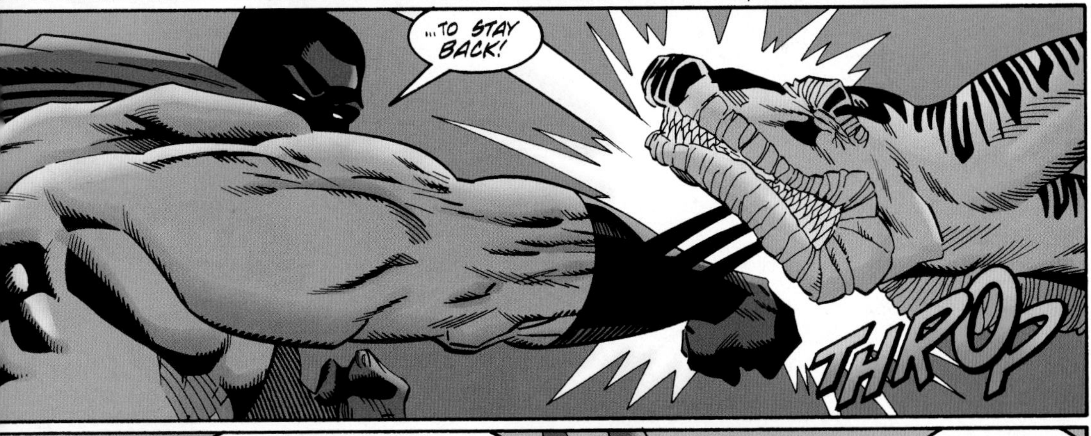
...TO STAY BACK!
THROP

HE'S DOWN, SIR--BUT THERE ARE OTHERS!
HIS FOLLOWERS IN THE HOODED CLOAKS!
OPHILIATORS, ALFRED--BRAINWASHED ZOMBIES...

"THEIR MINDS ARE APPARENTLY CONTROLLED BY THE SILENT VIBRATION OF ALIEN CRYSTAL..."
...BUT WHEN THOSE VIBRATIONS ARE OUT OF RANGE--OR STILLED...
deet
BWHOOM
...THE OPHIOLATORS FALL CATATONIC--COLLAPSING LIKE CLIPPED PUPPETS.
THEN... IT'S OVER, SIR--YOU STOPPED THEM, AND MADE IT SEEM EASY.
I WAS WRONG TO WORRY THAT YOU MIGHT NOT BE--
A TUNNEL, SIR, FROM THIS CAVE ALL THE WAY TO OURS.
WHAT ARE YOU DOING HERE, ALFRED? HOW DID OPHIDIAN GET YOU?
I SUGGEST SEALING BOTH ENDS--AFTER THIS NEST OF VIPERS IS CLEANED OUT.
ALL THESE BONES, ALFRED--ALL THE CITY'S MISSING PERSONS...

OPHIDIAN MUST RANK AS THE GREATEST MASS MURDERER IN GOTHAM'S HISTORY, BUT...
BUT WHAT, SIR?
EVERY BONE IS STRIPPED CLEAN... SO WHAT HAS BECOME OF ALL THAT FLESH?

POLICE HEADQUARTERS:
YOU DIDN'T BURN HIM.
NO NEED, COMMISSIONER...

HE WAS SOMEHOW CONTROLLED BY EMANATIONS FROM THE METEOR-CRYSTAL-- THE OPHITE...
THE SINGING IS STILLED... AND I HEAR ONLY SILENCE.
ANCIENT ONES, WHY HAVE YOU FORSAKEN ME...?

NOW THAT THIS EXTERNAL INFLUENCE HAS BEEN REMOVED--
YOU'RE ARGUING AGAINST EXECUTION?
GIVE ME A MATCH-- AND I'LL BURN HIM.
QUIET, OFFICER KNIGHT.

JEREMY ADDER WAS CHOSEN.
HE'S A VICTIM.
IF SO, IT'S BECAUSE HE WAS ALREADY EVIL.
THE DARK LORDS DON'T POSSESS INNOCENTS--
--THEY KILL THEM TO HUNT THE GHOSTS, TO CORRUPT AND DEVOUR THE SOULS.

I'M NOT SAYING HE'S INNOCENT, COMMISSIONER.
HAVEN'T HEARD YOU SAY HE'S GUILTY.
OF COURSE HE IS--BUT GUILTY OF WHAT?
OF ATROCITY...
"YOU FOUND THAT PIT OF SKELETONS! THINK OF ALL THOSE NAKED SOULS FLEEING THROUGH DARK HORROR--
"--ALL BECAUSE OF JEREMY ADDER."
BUT DID HE TRANSFORM HIMSELF INTO A SNAKE, COMMISSIONER?
DID HE CHOOSE TO LOSE HIS MIND? HIS WILL? HIS HUMANITY?
SILENCE IS NOT GOLDEN... BUT EMPTY DROSS.
YOU'RE SAYING WE SHOULD PITY HIM?
CONTAIN HIM.
STUDY HIM.
MAYBE LEARN ABOUT HIS MASTERS.
COME TO GRIPS WITH THE REAL EVIL, FOR WHICH HE WAS A TOOL--KNOW OUR TRUE ENEMY.
YOU MEAN KEEP HIM ALIVE--IN SOME SORT OF... ASYLUM?
YES--FOR THE CRIMINALLY POSSESSED.
...SOME OR ALL OF WHOM MAY HOLD THE KEY TO UNLOCK GOTHAM'S SALVATION.

BUT WHERE? WHAT LOCKS HIM AWAY FROM HIS VICTIMS?
MY FATHER OWNED PROPERTY OUT ON OLD ARKHAM ROAD...
YOU'RE SERIOUS?
IT'S BETTER THAN KILLING HIM.
HE AND HIS KIND KILL EVERY NIGHT!
AND WHEN WE BECOME THEM, OFFICER KNIGHT-- WHEN WE JOIN IN THE KILLING--OUR FATE IS SEALED.
HE'S WRONG, SIR! THERE ARE TWO TYPES OF PEOPLE IN THIS HAUNTED CITY--THE EVIL AND THE INNOCENT-- THOSE WHOM THE DARK LORDS USE, AND THOSE WHOM THEY PREY UPON!
AND THEN, OFFICER KNIGHT... THERE'S THE BATMAN.
BUT HE'S CRAZY, SIR!
NO.
OPHIDIAN IS CRAZY... EMIL VARNER WAS CRAZY.
THE BATMAN MAY BE OBSESSED...
"...BUT HE'S HARDLY INSANE.
"IF ANYTHING, HIS MIND HAS BEEN SO FINELY TOOLED... IT OPERATES LIKE A MACHINE."
BUT EVEN THOUGH IT'S FINISHED, WITH OPHIDIAN AND HIS FOLLOWERS CAPTURED...
STILL FEELS IMPOSSIBLE FOR EVIL'S INFLUENCE TO REACH SO FAR THROUGH THE COSMOS.

...IT DOESN'T FEEL FINISHED.
SH-KAK-A-LAK
WH-WHAT ...?
THE BONES... THEY'RE M-MOVING!
TOO MUCH MYSTERY REMAINS, TOO MANY UNANSWERED QUESTIONS.
YAHH! LOOK OUT!
BRRUK
PWSHSHSH
WERE THE OPHILIATORS CANNIBALS? DID THEY EAT ALL OF GOTHAM'S MISSING PERSONS?
IF NOT, WHY WERE ALL THE SKELETONS STRIPPED CLEAN?
WHAT HAPPENED TO THE FLESH OF--
DOWN THERE, IN THE BURSTING STREET-- THE ANSWERS.
RISING UP FROM HELL ITSELF...

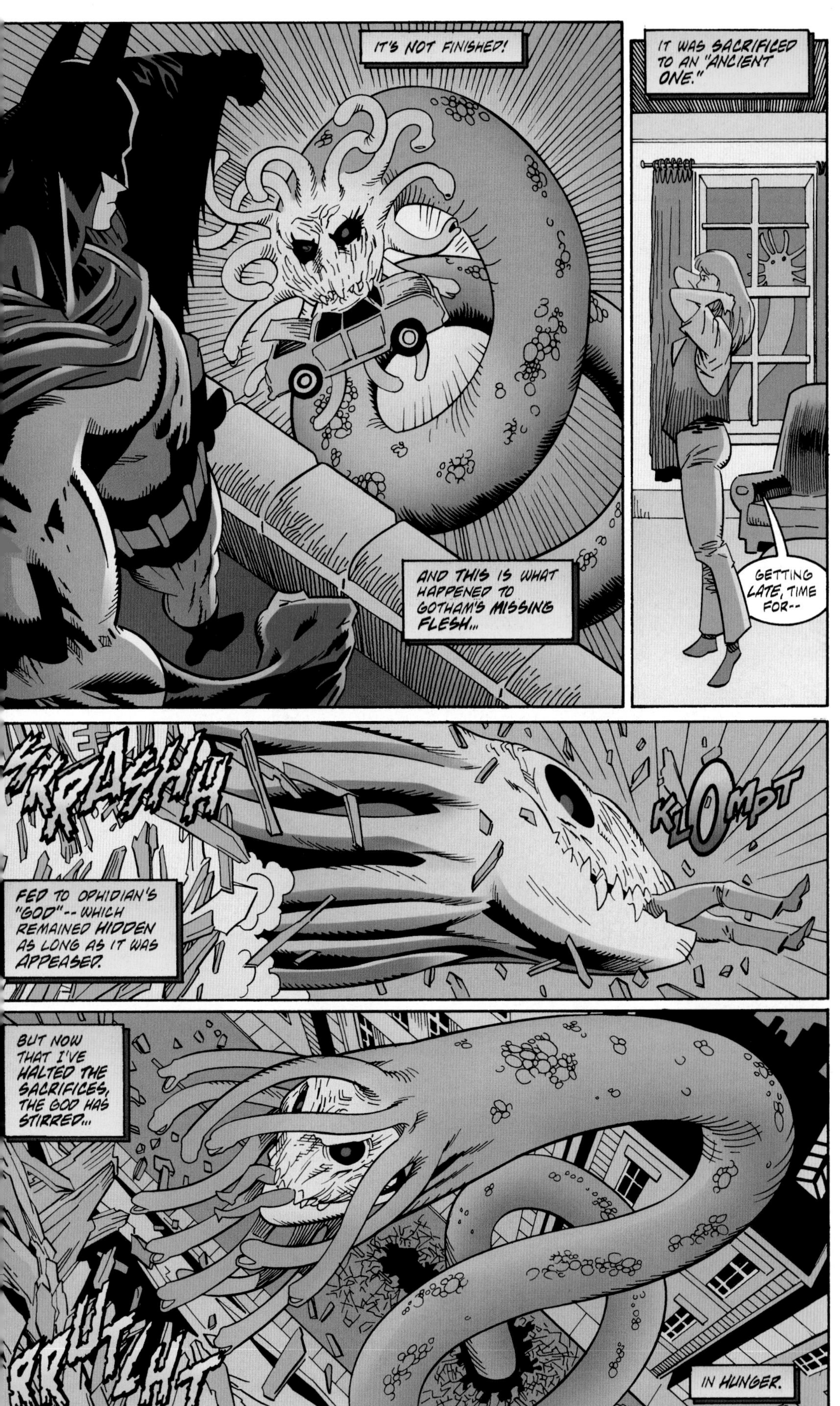
IT'S NOT FINISHED!
IT WAS SACRIFICED TO AN "ANCIENT ONE."
AND THIS IS WHAT HAPPENED TO GOTHAM'S MISSING FLESH...
GETTING LATE, TIME FOR--
SKRASHH
KLOMPT
FED TO OPHIDIAN'S "GOD"-- WHICH REMAINED HIDDEN AS LONG AS IT WAS APPEASED.
BUT NOW THAT I'VE HALTED THE SACRIFICES, THE GOD HAS STIRRED...
RRUUTCHT
IN HUNGER.

GOT TO MOVE FAST.
GOT TO REACH--

--GORDON.
SEVEN BLOCKS AWAY, KNIGHT, AND IT STILL LOOKS ENORMOUS! WE NEED--
OUR OWN VENOM, COMMISSIONER...

ENOUGH POISON TO STOP THAT THING--AND A MEANS OF DELIVERING THE POISON TO THE MONSTER'S MOST VULNERABLE POINT.
THAT'S WHAT WE NEED TO HALT THIS FEEDING FRENZY--AND WE NEED IT NOW.

NINETEEN MINUTES LATER:
HERE.
BEST MY PEOPLE COULD DO ON SUCH SHORT NOTICE--BUT IT JUST MIGHT WORK.

CORROSIVE ACID RATHER THAN POISON.
SHORT NEEDLE.
I'LL HAVE TO REACH AN EYE.

GOOD LUCK.
GODSPEED.
DOES THAT MEAN YOU STILL TRUST ME?
DO I HAVE ANY CHOICE?
NOT UNLESS YOU WANT TO FLY.
AT LEAST THE WIND'S WITH ME, BLOWING STRAIGHT TOWARD THE SERPENT.
AND THE BAT-WINGS WORK PERFECTLY, AS I KNEW THEY WOULD.
IF MY FATHER HAD NOT TESTED THE WINGS BEFORE HIS DEATH, THEY WOULD NEVER HAVE BEEN STOWED IN THE CAR-- FOR ME TO FIND AFTER HIS DEATH.
NOW-- TIME TO RELEASE...

"ENTER THE SNAKE," SAID THE GHOST OF MY FATHER, "AND SLAY ITS HEART."
I THOUGHT I HAD ALREADY DONE SO, BUT I WAS WRONG.
THE SNAKE I PREVIOUSLY ENTERED WAS A FALSE ONE--MADE OF COLD STONE SENT FROM DISTANT STARS.
BUT THIS TIME THE SNAKE IS REAL--AND I CAN HEAR THE PULSE OF ITS LIFE.
IT'S POUNDING LOUDEST NEAR THAT WOMAN--SWALLOWED WHOLE AND STILL ALIVE.
Ohhh...
INJURED AND DELIRIOUS, BUT NOT YET DIGESTED.
HERE.
SHRRRPT
ON THE OTHER SIDE OF THIS MEMBRANE...
THE SERPENT'S HUGE HEART--
GLSHT
--THE ENGINE PUMPING ITS FOUL BLOOD... ITS STRONGEST ORGAN AND GREATEST WEAKNESS.

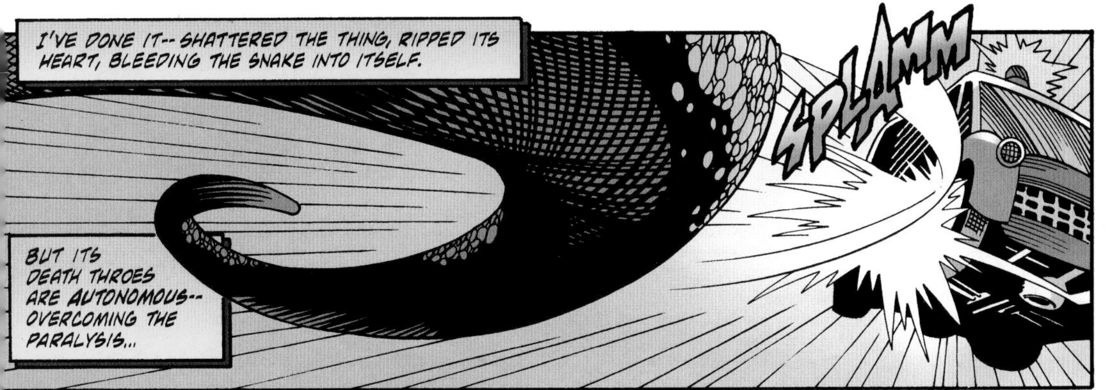
I'VE DONE IT-- SHATTERED THE THING, RIPPED ITS HEART, BLEEDING THE SNAKE INTO ITSELF.
SPLAMM
BUT ITS DEATH THROES ARE AUTONOMOUS-- OVERCOMING THE PARALYSIS...

...THRASHING AND TUMBLING US THROUGH THE LENGTH OF ITS BODY, THE DURATION OF ITS DEATH.
WUDT
CAN'T LOSE CONSCIOUSNESS--CAN'T DROWN IN THE BLOOD PUMPING FROM ITS SLASHED HEART...

TRASHED YOUR VAN, COMMISSIONER, BUT IT'S FINALLY DYING--FALLING STILL.
YES, OFFICER KNIGHT--BUT ONLY AFTER THE BATMAN ENTERED ITS MOUTH...

THEN...SOMEHOW HE...HE KILLED IT FROM WITHIN.
AND DIED DOING IT...OFFERING ONE LAST SACRIFICE TO OPHIDIAN'S HELLISH GOD.
HIMSELF.

WAIT, COMMISSIONER! IT'S OPENING ITS MOUTH--COMING BACK TO LIFE!
NO--IT'S STILL DEAD, OFFICER KNIGHT...
"...BUT HE'S NOT!"
NEVER TRUST DEATH, COMMISSIONER GORDON--NOT IN HAUNTED GOTHAM.
AND WITH THAT IN MIND, I SUGGEST YOU CHOP THIS SERPENT INTO A THOUSAND PIECES.
FEED EVERY PIECE THROUGH A WOOD-CHIPPER.
BOIL THE REMAINS UNTIL THE GRUE STEAMS OFF.
INCINERATE WHAT'S LEFT.
PULVERIZE THE ASHES.
THEN WAIT FOR A STRONG WIND--AND SCATTER THEM.
MAYBE, JUST FOR A MOMENT OR TWO... THEY'LL SCREEN OUT THE STARS.

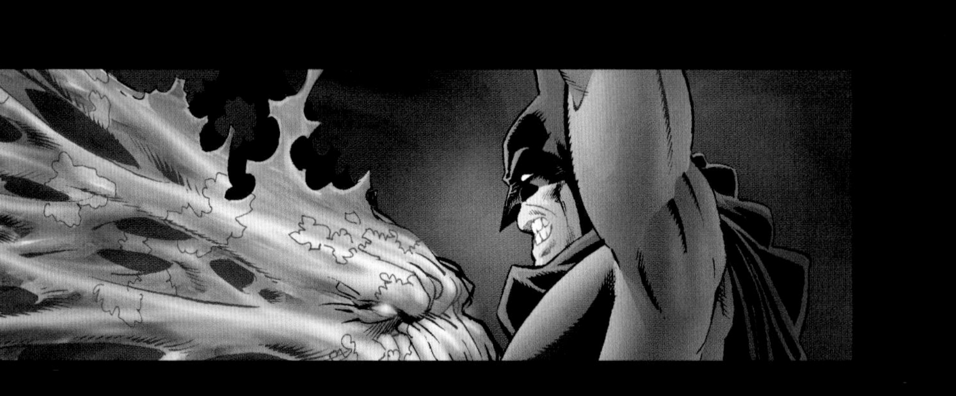

LREADY POWERFUL ENOUGH TO TAIN EVERY SOUL IN GOTHAM, HE DARK LORDS GROW TRONGER BY THE NIGHT, KILLING HE LIVING TO FEED ON THE EAD AND INCREASING THEIR OTENCY WITH EACH SOUL ONSUMED.
ONE VICTIM AT A TIME, THE ENTIRE CITY IS GOING TO HELL.
MY VOW: STOP IT OR DIE TRYING-- EVEN IF IT MEANS FEEDING THE EVIL WITH MY OWN SOUL.
SUCCEED ONCE AND FOR ALL, OR FAIL DOUBLY.
SWERVE AWAY FROM HELL, OR CRASH FASTER.
HAUNTED GOTHAM — PART FOUR
BLOOD OF THE BAT
SOME VOW.

WAYNE MANOR:
TO KEEP IT, I'LL NEED HELP.
AND HELP I HAVE SUMMONED...

NOBLE SOULS, EVERY ONE, THE KIND MOST PRIZED BY THE DARK LORDS--WHOSE FAVORED VICTIMS ARE THOSE WHO LEAST DESERVE TO DIE, AND WHO MUST BE CORRUPTED AFTER DEATH BEFORE FUELING THE GREATER EVIL.
MOTHER, I WILL FIND YOU, AND I WILL SAVE YOU.
THIS I SWEAR

EVEN IF SHE'S STILL FREE, BRUCE...

...THEY'RE HUNTING HER IN A CLOSED PRESERVE.
MY FATHER'S GHOST--DOOMED TO SEEK HIS DEAD WIFE AND HAUNT HIS LIVING SON, EVEN AS HE FLEES DEMONS BENT ON DRAGGING HIM DOWN.
THEY'RE GETTING CLOSER, BRUCE, AND TIME IS THE ENEMY.

LIKE ME--AND ALL THE DEAD--YOUR MOTHER IS BARRED FROM ESCAPE.
THE DARK LORDS HAVE CUT OFF THE PATH TO HEAVEN--AND SEALED IT.
IF SHE IS NOT LOCATED SOON--
TONIGHT, FATHER--I'VE MADE ARRANGEMENTS TO ENSURE IT.
BUT BEFORE I VENTURE ANY FARTHER ON THIS COURSE CHARTED FOR ME--BY YOU--I MUST KNOW MORE ABOUT WHAT I'VE BECOME.
ABOUT... THE BAT.

THE BAT IS HAUNTED GOTHAM'S ONLY HOPE, BRUCE.
YOU'VE BECOME THE SCOURGE OF THE DARK LORDS-- THIS CITY'S SAVIOR.
BUT WHY MUST A SAVIOR ASSUME SUCH DARK DESIGN?
ON THE NIGHT YOU AND MOTHER WERE ASSASSINATED, BEFORE THE DESIGN WAS EVEN REVEALED...

"...THE SKELETON NAMED CAL SAID ONE WORD TO ME-- AND THE WORD WAS 'BATS.'"
WELP, HERE WE ALL ARE.

"AND WHEN I LATER ASKED POLICE COMMISSIONER GORDON WHY YOU CHOSE A BAT AS MY DESTINY, HE SAID YOU HAD RECEIVED SOME 'SIGN.'
HERE WE ALL ARE INDEED--GATHERED, I SUSPECT, FOR ONE HELL OF A PARTY.
WITHOUT HEAVEN, COMMISSIONER, WHAT OTHER KIND IS THERE?

WHAT "SIGN," FATHER?
I... I'VE NEVER TOLD ANYONE, BRUCE... NOT EVEN YOUR MOTHER...
BUT AS YOU SAY, FATHER, TIME IS SHORT.
SO TELL ME-- NOW.

V-VERY WELL.
THE SIGN WAS... INSPIRATION... AND IT DICTATED NOT JUST YOUR FATE, BUT SHAPED YOUR ENTIRE LIFE OF STUDY AND TRAINING...
HOW COULD IT DO THAT?
IT... IT WAS THE NIGHT OF YOUR BIRTH, SON, UPSTAIRS IN THIS VERY MANOR...

"THE NIGHT OF YOUR BIRTH. BUT THE BEGINNING OF A LONG, SLOW DEATH FOR THE INVISIBLE COLLEGE.
"WE WERE SWORN TO EXORCISE GOTHAM, AND YET ONE OF OUR OWN--EMIL VARNER--DARED TO PRACTICE VILE SORCERY IN THE VERY SANCTITY OF WAYNE MANOR...
GET OUT, VARNER--NOW!
"IT CAME IN THROUGH THE FALL WINDOW, SHOWERING ME WITH GLASS...
KRSSH
SKREEEEEEE
"...HAMMERING MY HEART.
"FEARING THE END OF EVERYTHING ON THAT NIGHT OF YOUR BEGINNING, I CHASED THE THING UP THE MAIN STAIRS...
"IT WAS HOVERING ABOVE YOUR CRIB--A HELLISH CREATURE OF RED EYES AND BLACK WINGS, FAR LARGER THAN A NORMAL BAT.
"AND THEN, ALTHOUGH IT WAS UTTERLY IMPOSSIBLE--

"...A WORKING DESIGNED TO INCREASE PERSONAL POWER BY ABSORBING THE VIRGIN SOUL OF A SLAIN NEWBORN.
"I LATER LEARNED THAT HIS SPELL WOULD HAVE BEEN AIMED AT YOU, SON...
"HAD I KNOWN, I MIGHT HAVE KILLED VARNER THEN AND THERE.
"AS IT WAS, I BROODED LATE IN THE LIBRARY, PONDERING THE INCIDENT AS THE WORST POSSIBLE OMEN TIMED TO YOUR BIRTH, AND PRAYING FOR SOME COUNTERING SIGN...
"...AND, IN FRANTIC HORROR, DOWN THE LONG HALL TO THE ROOM WHOSE SHADOWS HELD MY DEFENSELESS WIFE AND SON.
"INSIDE, YOUR EXHAUSTED MOTHER WAS IN DEEP SLEEP, BUT THE SIGN, BRUCE...
"--THE THING SPOKE...
I AM THE BAT.
"...AS DID YOU.
AND I AM THE MAN.

TOGETHER WE SHAPE THE DARK DESTINY OF HAUNTED GOTHAM'S SAVIOR.

"AND THEN THE CREATURE WAS GONE, LOST IN THE DARK, AND SOMEHOW I WAS HOLDING YOU, SPELLBOUND BY YOUR TOO-KNOWING EYES."

TEACH ME, FATHER, TRAIN ME...

PREPARE ME TO WITH-STAND ALL THE FIRES OF HELL.

AFTER THAT, YOU SAID NOTHING FOR ELEVEN MONTHS--AND THEN, YOUR "FIRST" WORD WAS NEITHER "DAD" NOR "MOM"...
IT WAS... "BAT."
YOU'RE SAYING I ASKED FOR IT?

ASKED FOR THIS?
I'M SAYING YOUR DARK DESTINY WAS SHAPED NOT BY ME, BUT BY A SIGN...
...AND THAT "SIGN" WAS AN AWESOME CREATURE OF THE NIGHT.

BUT WHO SENT THE SIGN? WHERE DID THE GIANT BAT COME FROM? WHERE DID IT GO? WHAT MADE THE BABY SPEAK?
I DON'T KNOW, BRUCE, BUT IF GOTHAM IS HAUNTED BY EVIL FORCES...
...THEN PERHAPS IT IS ALSO TOUCHED BY A FORCE OF GOOD.
MAYBE THIS BIZARRE "BAT-MAN" PERSONA IS NOTHING BUT A TRAP--INTO WHICH YOU DRAGGED YOUR NEWBORN SON.
OR THE SAME EVIL FORCE, FATHER, PLAYING A GAME.
A TRICK.
I'VE PONDERED THAT POSSIBILITY LONG AND HARD--
...THROUGH ALL THE YEARS OF YOUR YOUTH...
...AND WHILE IT DOES NOT FEEL TRUE, YOU SHOULD REMAIN AWARE OF IT.
...THIS MANTLE OF THE BAT SEEMING TO CONFER A STRANGELY SEDUCTIVE POWER.
TO OPPOSE GOTHAM'S EVIL, FIGHTING FIRE WITH FIRE, YOU MUST CLOAK YOURSELF IN DARKNESS--BUT NEVER SUCCUMB TO ITS LURE.
IT DOES TEMPT ME, FATHER...
BUT USED THUS FAR ONLY FOR GOOD?
IF NOT FOR GOOD, AT LEAST FOR OPPOSING EVIL.

THEN THE POWER DERIVES NOT FROM MANTLE OR MASK, MY SON, BUT FROM YOU.
JUST RESIST THE TEMPTATION... BETTER THAN I DID.
WHAT DO YOU--
MASTER BRUCE?
YES, ALFRED.
THE GUESTS HAVE ARRIVED, SIR, AND ARE ASSEMBLED FOR THE SEANCE--
"--IN THE LIBRARY."
R. PICKMAN
ONCE I'VE ENTERED THE TRANCE STATE...
...WHATEVER HAPPENS, DO NOT BREAK CONTACT.
EVEN IF YOU'RE IN DISTRESS, CAT MAJIK?
UNDER PSYCHIC ATTACK?
IF THAT HAPPENS, BAT-MAN... BREAKING THE SEANCE COULD SEVER MY LINK TO MORTAL LIFE.

ONCE WE'VE GATHERED AROUND THE TABLE, FORMING A CIRCLE OF TOUCHING HANDS, WE MUST HOLD FAST AND HANG TIGHT--NO MATTER WHAT HAPPENS.
THIS IS CRUCIAL.
WITHOUT OUR COMBINED PSYCHIC ENERGIES, I CAN NEITHER REACH THE SPIRITUAL PLANE NOR RETURN TO THIS REALM.
AND AFTER I HAVE OPENED THE WAY, YOU MAY BE SHOCKED BY WHAT OCCURS.
YOU MAY EVEN BE TERRIFIED.
I DON'T CARE.
MY LIFE WILL BE LITERALLY IN YOUR HANDS.
DO NOT LET GO OF IT.
NOW LET'S TAKE OUR SEATS AND ANNOUNCE OURSELVES BEFORE WE BEGIN, SHALL WE?

I AM CAT MAJIK. THE MEDIUM THROUGH WHICH THIS SEANCE WILL BE CONDUCTED.
JAMES GORDON, POLICE COMMISSIONER OF THIS CURSED CITY.
SIMON STEELE, VICAR OF STILLWATER, THE ONLY CHURCH REMAIN-ING IN GOTHAM.
OFFICER CASSANDRA KNIGHT--UNDERCOVER AND UNDERPAID COP.
ALFRED PENNYWORTH, GENTLEMAN'S GENTLEMAN AND KEEPER OF WAYNE MANOR.
CAL-- SIDEWALK SHILL FOR A JOINT CALLED THE BONEYARD.
THE BATMAN.
SON OF THOMAS AND MARTHA WAYNE, NOW DECEASED.
SECRET WEAPON OF THE INVISIBLE COLLEGE, NOW DEFUNCT.
THANK YOU-- AND NOW--LET IT BEGIN...LET OUR ENERGIES UNITE TO OPEN THE WAY...
YES, WILD WINDS FROM THE OTHER SIDE CHILLING MY HEART... SWEEPING THROUGH THE CONDUIT OF MY SOUL...
NOT TO MENTION THE COLD DRAFT IN THIS ROOM...
QUIET, OFFICER KNIGHT!

chlnktnkklnk
BUT SHE'S RIGHT, COMMISH!
WHOLE CHANDELIER'S SWAYIN'...AND THE TABLE'S MOVIN', TOO!
IGNORE IT! REMEMBER HER ADMONISHMENT!
DON'T BREAK CONTACT!
THE TRANCE DEEPENS... AS THE WINDS BEAR OTHER SOULS...THE SPIRITS OF THE DEAD AND--
AUGH-K! WE GOT YOUR MOTHER, BRUCIE-BOY! TASTY WOMAN, AS YOU KNOW-- SOUL AS PURE AS THE FLEECE OF A LAMB BEFORE SLAUGHTER...
...OR AT LEAST IT WAS--BEFORE WE STARTED SPICING IT.
WHERE IS SHE? WHERE IS MY MOTHER?!
SHE'S DEAD, YOU IDIOT!
BUT HER GHOST IS RIGHT HERE, BEING TORTURED BY DEMONS RIGHT NOW!
IF YOU HAD ANY GUTS, YOU'D KILL YOURSELF AND TRY TO SAVE HER!
NO! I--
DON'T LISTEN TO IT!

JUST HOLD FAST-- UNTIL WE FIND HER!
FIND HER HOW? THROUGH THIS SHAPE-SHIFTING GYPSY-TRASH CAT-MAJIK?!
CAT MAJIK COULDN'T FIND A DAMNED DEMON IN HELL!
SHE'S A DABBLER AND A FRAUD, AND A FOOL!
SHE CAME LOOKING FOR YOUR MOTHER--
--BUT OPENED THE WAY FOR US!
THE EVIL SPIRITS-- STREAKING AWAY!
I'M HERE-- AND I'LL DO ANYTHING! JUST TELL ME HOW TO HELP YOU!
I'VE ALREADY BEEN DARKENED, PERVERTED, AND THE DARK LORDS ARE COMING TO FEAST EVEN NOW... TO DEVOUR MY SOUL, ADDING MY STRENGTH TO THEIRS...
TOO LATE, FOOLISH BOY!

SHAPE-SHIFTING?
WE'RE INSIDE THE BLIND SEER RIGHT NOW-- AND WE'RE NOT IMPRESSED!
GOOD LORD!
LET THEM GO!
YOU'RE DOOMED, BRUCE-- A THING OF DARKNESS, DAMNED AND DOOMED!
M-MOTHER!
DON'T BREAK THE CIRCLE! I'M CLOSE! I CAN SEE SOMEONE... THROUGH THE MISTS...RUSHING FORWARD... AND IT... IT'S YOUR MOTHER--!
THERE IS NO HOPE, NO SALVATION-- NOT HERE, NOT IN GOTHAM!
YOU'RE WRONG, MOTHER!
NO! THERE MUST BE SOME WAY TO--
THERE IS NO WAY! I'M NOTHING BUT THE HEART OF A LION-- SOUL-FODDER--FUEL FOR THEIR POWER!
DON'T GIVE IN, MOTHER! YOU AND FATHER AND THE OTHERS IN THE INVISIBLE COLLEGE WERE THE ONLY ONES WHO EVER STOPPED THEIR PREDATIONS!
YOU PREVENTED MURDERS AND SOUL-THEFT!
AND LOOK WHERE IT GOT US! MURDERED BY A WEREWOLF ASSASSIN AND HUNTED THROUGH HELL!
FACE IT, BRUCE, WE WERE ONLY DELAYING THE INEVITABLE!
IN THE END, THE INVISIBLE COLLEGE CREATED NOTHING BUT EMIL VARNER, A LOT OF DEATH, AND YOU...
...A PATHETIC "BAT-MAN" CRYING IN THE DARK FOR HIS LOST MOMMY!

A MOMMY YOU'LL NEVER HAVE AGAIN, YOU BAD LITTLE BOY, AFTER I'VE BEEN DEVOURED BY THE DARK LORDS!
AGENTS OF EVIL WITH GREEDY HEARTS AND SHARP TEETH!
AND HERE THEY COME, SONNY-BOY, CLOSING IN ON ME RIGHT NOW...
RUN FROM THEM, MOTHER!
COME HERE!
THROUGH CAT MAJIK!
COME TO ME!
UH... BRUCE? IS THAT REALLY WISE?
CAL'S RIGHT-- THIS COULD BE A BIG MISTAKE, EVEN A TRAP.
IF YOUR MOTHER'S SOUL IS TURNING EVIL, THEN INVITING IT HERE, INTO YOUR MANOR--
IS HER ONLY HOPE!
HER ONLY POSSIBLE ESCAPE ROUTE!
YES, BUT IT COULD UNDO EVERYTHING! THE MANOR WAS PROTECTED BY SPELLS, BUT IF YOU LET THE EVIL IN--
WHAT SPELLS, GORDON?
WE'VE ALREADY OPENED THE WAY--FROM WITHIN--FOR A HALF-DOZEN SPIRITS TO CROSS OVER...!
"THEY'RE LOOSE IN THE MANOR RIGHT NOW--AND IF YOUR MOTHER JOINS THEM, THEY COULD WIELD ENOUGH POWER TO OPEN THE WAY FROM WITHOUT."
TO WAYNE MANOR AND ITS SEVEN LIVES! SEVEN HUSKS OF MEAT FOR US-- SEVEN SOULS FOR OUR MASTERS!

THIS MANOR WAS PROTECTED BY WHAT SPELLS--?
YOU TOLD ME MY FATHER WAS NOT A SORCERER!
I ALSO TOLD YOU THE SECRET SIX WERE COMMITTED TO FIGHTING FIRE WITH FIRE--
--AND THAT MEANT HELL-FIRE, I'M SORRY TO SAY.
JUST RESIST THE TEMPTATION,, BETTER THAN I DID.
YOUR FATHER ALWAYS WAS WEAK!
ALFRED?
HE SUCCUMBED TO THE DARK ARTS BUT ONCE, SIR, AND REGRETTED IT EVER AFTER...BUT THIS MANOR HAD TO BE AN INVIOLABLE SANCTUARY.
THE PROTECTIONS HAVE ALREADY BEEN BREACHED BY CAT MAJIK'S CONDUIT TO THE OTHER REALM-- AND BRINGING YOUR MOTHER ACROSS COULD SHATTER THE SPELLS COMPLETELY...
...MAYBE EVEN OPEN THE WAY FOR THE DARK LORDS THEMSELVES TO--
LET THEM COME! I WANT MY MOTHER'S SOUL HERE--NOW--WHERE I CAN AT LEAST TRY TO PROTECT HER!
GUAGH-K
YOU ASKED FOR IT, BRUCIE-BOY... AND NOW YOU'LL HAVE ALL HELL TO FACE AND PAY, YOU SIMPERING BRAT!
MOTHER--!

SHUT UP, BRUCE! I'VE HAD ENOUGH!
HUAHH
CONSIDER YOURSELF WEANED AND SHOVED FROM THE NEST!
YOU'RE ON YOUR OWN NOW, READY OR NOT--
--AND YOU'RE IN A WHOLE NEW WORLD OF TERRIBLE TROUBLE.
MOTHER!
AHN--!
THE CIRCLE... B-BROKEN...
CAT MAJIK! ARE YOU ALL RIGHT?
Y-YES, BUT... THE BAT IS IN EXTREME DANGER... MADE VULNERABLE BY THE VERY THING HE SEEKS TO SAVE...

BY HIS MAMA.
IF YOU CAN CALL IT HIS MOTHER.
HE'S GONE--BROKE THE CIRCLE TO PURSUE THE GHOST...
AND WE MUST PURSUE HIM--BEFORE THE GHOST LURES HIM INTO DOOM.
COME ON--SPLIT UP AND SEARCH THE ENTIRE MANOR...
FIND THE BAT BEFORE HE FINDS HER.
QUICKLY!
THE DARK LORDS COMMAND MANY AGENTS, AND WITH THIS MANOR COMPROMISED--
"--WE MAY SOON SUFFER ATTACK FROM WITHIN AND WITHOUT--BY ALL THE DEAD OF GOTHAM!"
MASTER BRUCE! COME BACK, SIR! WHERE ARE--
--YAHH!

H-HELLLLL
T-TRAPPED IN THE PAINTING?
GOOD LORD! GOT TO FIND SOME WAY OUT...
GOT TO FIND THE MASTER ...!
OR HIS MOTHER!
WELL, THAT'S ONE GONE.
OVER THE HILL AND OUT OF THE PICTURE--FOREVER.
HYAH! LET'S GET THE OTHERS!

THE BILLIARDS ROOM:
FREEZE!
OR YOU'LL DO WHAT--?

SHOOT US?
BAM
BAM
BAM

HYAHAHAHAHAHA
WUD
TUD
Uhn!

THE KITCHEN:
YO, WAYNE!
BATMAN!
YOU IN HERE?

WHA--?
WT

STOK
TUNK
TOK
YAOW!

THE CAVE:

MARTHA, N-NO!

WHY NOT, THOMAS? IF I CAN'T SCARE OUR SON AS A GHOST...

...MAYBE MY POSSESSE CORPSE WIL TURN THE TRICK!

P-PLEASE, MARTHA!

SHUT UP, YOU HELPLESS FOOL!

BUT...

JUST HIDE IF YOU KNOW WHAT'S GOOD FOR YOU THANK TO OUR DOLTISH SON'S SEANCE...

...THIS MANOR IS NOW INFESTED WITH DEMONIC SPIRITS-- AND THEY'RE SEARCHING FOR YOU!

BLEEDING-HEART WRETCH-- ALWAYS OBSESSED WITH DUTY, THE INVISIBLE COLLEGE, HIS MEWLING SON... ANYTHING BUT ME...

DON'T
KNOW WHY
I EVER
MARRIED
HIM!
STAND ASIDE! I HAVE A MISSION TO COMPLETE.
YOU DO NOT FEAR US, ALFRED PENNYWORTH?
WHY SHOULD I? IF THIS IS THE REALM BEYOND--
--THEN YOU ARE MERE SPIRTS, AND CANNOT TOUCH ME!
AH, BUT WE CAN POSSESS YOU...
ONLY IF I GRANT YOU ENTRY THROUGH FEAR--AND WHILE I AM NEEDED BY MY MASTERS...
FWUFT
...I SHALL FEAR NO EVIL!
MY CLOAK--!
YOU WILL NEVER FIND YOUR WAY BACK!
I SHALL FIND MORE THAN THAT!
"I SHALL FIND MY MASTER--AND HIS MOTHER...
"...THE GOOD WOMAN I ONCE SERVED!"

THE PARLOR:
HEY, BRUCE--YOU HERE?
ANSWER ME IF YOU ARE, huh? TRUTH IS I'M GETTIN' KINDA CREEPED OUT BY--
eeps.
TO WAYNE MANOR.
SEVEN LIVES.
SEVEN HUSKS OF MEAT.
SEVEN SOULS.
THE WEST HALL, GROUND FLOOR:
MOTHER!
WHERE ARE Y-

CHUSH KEESH
GORDON WAS RIGHT.
PEESH KRSHH
MY FATHER'S PROTECTIVE SPELLS HAVE BEEN BROKEN...
SWUK
kritch
SKLOKT
...LEAVING THE MANOR OPEN TO ATTACK...
KRUKT
...FROM INSIDE AND OUT...
ruhrrrrrrrrrrrrrrRRAOWLL

CAT MAJIK?
NOW A SAVAGE WERE-BEAST--
--RIPPING THROUGH THE LAST OF THE DEAD.
THE SEANCE-SPIRIT WAS EVIL, BUT IT DID NOT LIE...
YOU ARE A SHAPE-SHIFTER.
AND YOU?
BECAUSE YOU ONLY PRETEND TO BE A BAT... ARE YOU PREJUDICED?
NO, BUT I PREFER YOU--
LIKE THIS?
HUMAN, YES-- A CAT-WOMAN IN NAME ONLY.
DIFFERENT MASKS FOR DIFFERENT TASKS-- AND HOWEVER YOU WANT ME...

GET BACK TO THE OTHERS! PROTECT THEM--AND IF IT CALLS FOR THE SKILLS OF A WERE-CAT, FEEL FREE TO SHIFT.
NOT NOW, CAT MAJIK.
NOT WITH MORE OF THE DEAD STILL GATHERING OUT THERE.
SOMETIMES... I HAVE NO CHOICE.
FARE YOU WELL, BAT-MAN--AND FOLLOW THE LIGHT.
SH-KLK
ALWAYS...
AND ONLY THE BRIGHTEST.
FROOOOOOSH
NOW...
OUT THE WINDOW AND UP TO THE ROOF--BEFORE ANY MORE REACH THE WINDOWS.

GOT TO HOLD OFF ALL EXTERNAL THREAT...

...BEFORE I CAN GO BACK INSIDE TO SEARCH THE MANOR.

AND FOR ONCE, IGNORANCE IS BLESSED.

HAD I KNOWN ABOUT MY FATHER'S WEAKNESS--HIS USE OF SORCERY--I MIGHT NEVER HAVE DUG THE MOAT, NOR FILLED IT WITH VOLATILE PITCH...

MY OWN "SPELL OF PROTECTION" SURROUNDING THE MANOR.
SWUFFF

FWOOOM

AND MY OWN VERSION OF FIGHTING FIRE WITH FIRE...

...BUT NO HELL ABOUT IT.

AGH-K! C-CAN'T...B-BREATHE!
BODY TO KILL!
FLESH TO EAT!
SOUL TO RELEASE!

SHHRRUT
-Hwuhh-

TH-
THANKS...
ANY MORE OF THEM, GORDON?
J-JUST... OUTSIDE.
THE FIRE WILL HOLD THEM BACK--

--AND WE HAVE AT LEAST AN HOUR BEFORE THE MOAT BURNS OUT.
ANY SIGNS OF MY MOTHER'S SPIRIT?
NONE.

THE OTHER GHOSTS WHO CROSSED OVER?
PROBABLY STILL INSIDE THE MANOR, BUT WHO KNOWS WHERE THEY--
KREEEEEK

WHAT THE--?
BEHIND ME, GORDON-- AND STAY BACK!

BAM BAM BAM
POK PUK PAK
FORGET THE GUN, OFFICER KNIGHT!
KLASHT
THERE'S NO FLESH AND BLOOD INSIDE THIS ARMOR!
KUSHT
AND EVEN SILVER BULLETS--
--CAN'T HARM--
KTUNK
SH-KLK
FROOOOSH
--A GHOST.

REEEAHH
BUT FIRE CAN.
MAKE A NOTE, CASSIE--STANDARD ISSUE FOR ALL OFFICERS FROM NOW ON...
FLAMETHROWERS.
YES, SIR.
NOW LET'S GET BACK TO THE OTHERS.
THINK, PENNYWORTH! EVEN IF I FIND THE MASTER'S MOTHER...
...HOW WILL I GET HER OUT OF THIS PLACE?
WHERE'S ALFRED PENNYWORTH?
DISAPPEARED--OR TAKEN, BY THE EVIL SPIRITS.
GPD
THE BAT JUST BURNED ONE OF THEM, BUT THE OTHERS ARE STILL AT LARGE.
ANY IDEA WHERE, CAL?
HEY, WHY ASK ME, COMMISH?
IT'S NOT LIKE I CAN FEEL 'EM IN MY BONES, Y'KNOW.

VICAR, YOU NEVER EXPLAINED WHY YOU WANTED THAT TANK.
QUITE SIMPLY, WE MAY WELL NEED A SECRET WEAPON BEFORE THIS NIGHT IS OUT.
WHAT SECRET WEAP--
UH, COMMISSIONER? I THOUGHT THE BAT WAS RIGHT BEHIND US, BUT--
GONE AGAIN? ALL RIGHT. THIS TIME WE ALL STAY TOGETHER UNTIL WE FIND HIM.
HE WAS BY THE SUIT-OF-ARMOR IN THE MAIN HALL--THE HUB OF THE ENTIRE MANOR--FROM WHICH HE COULD HAVE GONE ANYWHERE...
THE ONE PLACE I HAVEN'T LOOKED.
THE ONE ROOM I HAVEN'T EVEN ENTERED SINCE THE FUNERAL.
KREEEEEEEEEE
MY PARENTS' BEDROOM.

M-MOTHER ...?
OVER HERE, NAUGHTY CHILD... ON THE BED... WHERE YOU WERE CONCEIVED, LITTLE BRUCIE-BABE...
MAMA'S SISSY... ALWAYS MEWLING AND PULING, ALWAYS GRASPING AND CLINGING, ALWAYS FUSSING AND BEGGING TO BE SUCKLED... YOU GREEDY LITTLE GIT!

MOTHER, DON'T...
OH, NOW IT'S "MOTHER, DON'T," IS IT? BACK THEN, IT WAS ALWAYS "MOTHER, DO!"
MOTHER, DO THIS--MOTHER, DO THAT--MOTHER, DO EVERYTHING!
MOTHER, PLEASE--IT'S NOT YOU!
SOMETHING'S CHANGED YOU!

TRY DEATH, BRUCIE-BOY! THAT'LL CHANGE ANY LIVING THING!
THAT'LL ROT YOU RIGHT TO THE FOUL CORE!
YOU DON'T BELIEVE ME?
THEN COME AND SEE, BRUCIE-BOY! COME CLOSER...

COME SEE YOUR DEAR, SWEET MOMMY... PLUS HER SEVERAL THOUSAND SQUIRMING MAGGOTS, GIVE OR TAKE!
MOTHER, I WANT TO HELP YOU...
FROM WAY OVER THERE? HOW WILL YOU DO THAT, BRUCE?

COME CLOSER, COME TO MAMA, COME AND HELP ME...
BUT... IT'S A TRAP! IT'S NOT YOU, MOTHER! YOU'RE POSSESSED!

Y-YOU... YOU'RE RIGHT, BRUCE...
IT'S MY SOUL, BUT THEY'RE CORRUPTING IT...AND I...I CAN ONLY FIGHT THE DEMONS OFF FOR BRIEF PERIODS OF TIME...

...LIKE RIGHT NOW... BUT IT'S SO HARD...SUCH A STRAIN!

P-PLEASE, BRUCE, COME TO ME! I N-NEED YOUR STRENGTH... BEFORE THEY--
ALL RIGHT, MOTHER! I'M COMING!
AS I KNEW YOU WOULD, BRUCE...

BECAUSE YOU'RE SO MONUMENTALLY STUPID!
MOTHER, N-NO!
OH, YOU WANT TO DENY ME, YOU UNGRATEFUL BRAT?

AFTER ALL I'VE GIVEN YOU-- LIFE ITSELF--NOW YOU CAN'T FEED ME A LITTLE STRENGTH?
IT W-WAS A TRAP!

OF COURSE IT WAS, YOU THICK DOLT-- JUST AS YOU WERE A TRAP!

AN ACCIDENT! A MISTAKE!
Y-YOU'RE LYING!
AM I, BRUCE? HOW WOULD YOU KNOW? WERE YOU THERE?

BACK THEN, YOUR FATHER AND I WERE TOO BUSY WITH HIS PRECIOUS "INVISIBLE COLLEGE"--AND WHAT A JOKE THAT WAS! GOT US RIPPED TO SHREDS!
BUT BACK WHEN THE NOBLE COLLEGE STILL SEEMED LIKE A GOOD IDEA, WE DIDN'T HAVE TIME FOR A DISTRACTION LIKE YOU!
A CHILD IN GOTHAM! WHAT SENSE DOES THAT MAKE? FACE IT, BRUCIE-BOY--WE DIDN'T WANT YOU!
S-STOP IT, MOTHER!
AND NOW THAT YOU'RE HERE--UP CLOSE IN YOUR FULL GLORY-- I CAN SEE WHY!

WHO'D WANT TO GIVE BIRTH TO A BOUNCING BABY BAT?!
M-MOTHER... P-PLEASE...
OH, GROW UP YOU WHINING WEAKLING!
YOU ALWAYS WERE A SISSY!
AND IT WAS YOUR FATHER'S IDEA, NOT MINE, TO HARDEN YOU-- TO TURN THE MISTAKE INTO AN ASSET, SHAPE YOU INTO HIS TOOL, MOLD YOU TO HIS "DARK DESIGN"!
SHUT UP!
WHY, YOU INSOLENT WHELP, HOW DARE YOU?! YOU'D BEST TAKE A DEEP BREATH AND COUNT TO TEN, MISTER!
BETTER YET, TAKE A DEEP BREATH AND SMELL YOUR MOMMY! SMELL WHAT'S BECOME OF ME, THANKS TO YOU-- CORRUPT INSIDE AND OUT, BODY AND SOUL!
YOU LIKE MY FACE--?
KISS IT BETTER, BRUCIE-BOY! JOIN ME IN DARKNESS!
YOU'RE ALREADY A CREATURE OF THE NIGHT. YOU KNOW IT GIVES YOU POWER! SO JUST KISS ME AND...
SWUKK
NO!

MOTHER...
SHE'S GONE.
I'VE LOST HER.
SHE'S HERE--I'VE FOUND HER!
BUT SHE'S DEAD..
--AND THEREFORE OURS!
OUR THANKS, FOOL, FOR LEADING US TO HER RIPE FLESH.
HE'S NOT HERE, EITHER--NOTHING BUT THE SAME SEANCE SHAMBLES... SO HE MUST BE ON THE UPPER--
WAIT!
YES, I FEEL HIS ESSENCE... DIMINISHED... BUT--
YOU WERE RIGHT...

IT WAS A TRAP... AND I CAN'T SAVE HER... NOT WITHOUT SOME KIND OF HELP... NOT WHILE I'M ALIVE.
MAYBE I CAN HELP, BRUCE.
YOU, CAL? HOW?
WELL, IT'S LIKE GOOD NEWS AND BAD NEWS, SEE?
AND THE BAD NEWS IS ABOUT MY BONES, BRUCE, CUZ THEY'VE BEEN POSSESSED...
...FILLED WITH THE EVIL OF THOSE MISSING GHOSTS!
SWUD
WUP
TUD
BUT THE GOOD NEWS IS...
...THEY CAN HELP WITH YOUR PROBLEM OF BEING ALIVE!
KRTCH
BREAKING THE BONES DOES NO GOOD!
KRAKT
THE SPLINTERS JUST KEEP COMING--STILL POSSESSED!
SKSH
AND NOW, BRUCE, SHARP ENOUGH TO STAB!

UNLESS YOU PREFER BLUNT TRAUMA!
WOKT
STAND BACK! GIVE ME A CLEAR STREAM!
SPSHSHSHSH
THE WATER HAS BEEN BLESSED!

KLAK-A-LAK-TAK
TSSSSSSSS
YES--THE HOLY WATER IS DRIVING THE EVIL FROM THE BONES! BUT IT'S NOT DESTROYING THE SPIRITS! THEY'RE--

SORRY 'BOUT THAT, BRUCE, BUT I'M ALONE AGAIN NOW-- AND PRETTY MUCH BACK TO MY NORMAL SELF...

EXCEPT FOR THE REST OF MY FRAME BEING MULTIPLY FRACTURED.
IF I CAN DEAL WITH THE GHOST OF MY FATHER, CAL, YOU CAN DEAL WITH PLAYING YORICK.
YEAH, AT LEAST I'M ONE YORICK WHO CAN TALK BACK.
BUT IF YOU DON'T MIND, BRUCE, I'D PREFER A VANTAGE MORE COMMANDING THAN THE FLOOR.
MAYBE ON THE MANTEL OVER THERE...?
WHA--? THE PORTRAIT!
MY MOTHER-- GONE...LEAVING BLANK CANVAS!
WHOA.
BUT... HOW?
WHEN WE WERE INVADED FROM BEYOND, THIS ENTIRE MANOR BECAME MAGICKED! HOW MANY PAINTINGS HANG HERE?
I NEVER COUNTED-- A HUNDRED OR MORE.
THEN THERE ARE NOW A HUNDRED OR MORE WINDOWS TO THE REALM BEYOND--TO THE DOMAIN OF THE DARK LORDS.
AND THE DARK LORDS ARE HERE--ACTUALLY INSIDE THE MANOR?
TO RETRIEVE A PRIZE SO PRECIOUS, THEY WOULD VENTURE ANYWHERE.
AND TO HIDE FROM THEM, THE BAT'S MOTHER-- THE GOOD PART OF HER STILL REMAINING-- MAY HAVE TAKEN REFUGE IN THE PAINTINGS.

THEY'RE STILL AFTER ME--AND MY ARMS WEAKEN! CANNOT CARRY THE MISTRESS MUCH FARTHER BEFORE--
HERE, ALFRED! IN THE CAVE!
MISTER WAYNE! I'VE FOUND HER, SIR!
GOOD MAN, ALFRED! I'LL TAKE HER NOW!
BUT SHE IS SO STILL AND SO COLD, SIR, AND I... I FEAR THE WORST.
IF WE HAVE SERVED MY SON WELL, ALFRED, TAUGHT HIM TO BE STRONG AND RESOURCEFUL... THEN PERHAPS EVEN THE WORST NEED NOT BE FEARED.
SHE IS A CLEVER SPIRIT.
JUST AS THE DARK LORDS HAVE USED THE PAINTINGS TO CROSS OVER--
--SHE HAS RETREATED INTO THE SAME PAINTINGS TO HIDE.
BUT IF THE DARK LORDS HAVE INVADED THE MANOR, WHAT ARE THEY WAITING FOR? AND EXACTLY WHERE ARE--
BRUUMM
KRRAOOM
THE BASEMENT!
SHRASH

THEY'RE DOWN BELOW--SHAKING THE MANOR'S VERY FOUNDATIONS!
COME ON--AFTER HIM!
HEY, WHAT ABOUT ME?!
R. PICKMAN
IT AIN'T LIKE I CAN RUN, YA KNOW! I GOT NO FEMURS OR TIBIAS!
YOU'VE REUNITED US, ALFRED, AND YOUR WORK HERE IS DONE.
BUT... WHAT WILL YOU DO, SIR?
JUST AS MY BELOVED WIFE REFUSED TO ABANDON ME TO THE WEREWOLF ASSASSIN, SO DO I REFUSE TO ABANDON HER NOW.
I SHALL SEEK HER DELIVERANCE DEEPER IN THIS CAVE, ALFRED--BUT YOU'VE ALREADY DONE MORE THAN YOUR PART.
NOW GO.
FIND THE WAY BACK TO WAYNE MANOR BEFORE THEY FIND YOU.
I SHALL DO MY BEST, SIR.
AND MAY LIGHT SHINE UPON BOTH OF YOU.
THE ENTIRE MANOR--STILL QUAKING FROM BELOW! HURRY--WHILE WE KNOW WHERE THEY ARE! DOWN TO THE CAVE!
CAVE--?
THERE, GORDON! THROUGH THAT GRANDFATHER CLOCK!

MOTHER! FATHER!
LET GO OF ME, THOMAS. I HATE YOU-- YOU AND THE FOUL CHILD YOU MADE ME BEAR!

DON'T LISTEN TO HER LIES, SON! BEFORE SHE WAS POSSESSED, YOUR MOTHER LOVED YOU AS MUCH AS I!
NOW STOP IT, MARTHA! I'M TRYING TO SAVE YOU!

YOU HAVE ARRIVED, FALSE BAT, IN TIME TO WITNESS THE FEAST...
AND THERE IS NO WAY YOU CAN STOP US FROM DEVOURING YOUR MOTHER'S DARKENED SOUL!

MORE LIES, BRUCE! THERE IS A WAY TO STOP THE DEMONS FROM TAKING YOUR MOTHER!
BUT... HOW, FATHER?
YOU TAKE US--BEFORE THEY DO!

YOU'RE ASKING ME TO... NO! I... I CAN'T!
YOU MUST, SON! IT'S THE ONLY WAY--THE ONLY DELIVERANCE!

HAH! HE'S TOO WEAK!
HE COULDN'T BEAR TO SEE HIS PARENTS "MURDERED" A SECOND TIME--NOT BY HIS OWN HANDS!
DO IT, BRUCE-- NOW--WHILE THERE'S STILL TIME!

VICAR! YOU STILL HAVE HOLY WATER?
Y-YES, BUT... NOT NEARLY ENOUGH FOR SO MANY DEMONS...
NOT THE DEMONS, VICAR...

THE BATS!
SPRAY THEM! DRIVE THEM ABOVE MY PARENTS...

-NOW!"
SPSHSHSHSH
EEE
SKEE
EE
EEEE
MARTHA, DO YOU FEEL IT? FALLING FROM THE DARK WINGS...?
YES, THOMAS... LIKE SWEET RAIN FROM HEAVEN... HOLY WATER CLEANSING THE DARKNESS FROM MY SOUL...
FORGIVE ME, SON, FOR WHAT I WAS...
AND THANK YOU... FOR RESTORING WHAT I AM.
I LOVE YOU, AS I HAVE ALWAYS LOVED YOU, MORE THAN LIFE ITSELF.
NOW PLEASE... SAVE ME FROM THE DARK LORDS...AND WHAT THEY WOULD DO.
M-MOTHER... I...
SH-KLK
H-HOW CAN I... LOSE YOU AGAIN...?
TAKE THEM!
PERVERTED OR PURE, DEVOUR THEM BOTH--NOW!
DO IT, BRUCE! DON'T LET THEM TAKE US, SON! IN THE NAME OF ALL THAT'S HOLY...

DO IT NOWWWWW!
FROOOSH
NO--! THE SPIRITS --MADE MOLTEN!
...SPLASHING THE CARVED BAT!
YOU DARE DEPRIVE US OF--
FWHOOOOM
YOU DID IT! THE DARK LORDS ARE GONE--BANISHED BY THAT LIGHT FROM THE BAT...
THE LIGHT OF MY PARENTS' SACRIFICED SOULS, COMMISSIONER...
AND NOW... THEY ARE GONE, TOO.
BUT ONLY AFTER BEING REUNITED... AND REDEEMED.

HERE.
WAYNE MANOR...
KEEESH
THE MOAT'S BURNING OUT, BUT WITH NO DARK LORDS TO ATTRACT THEM, THE ZOMBIES HAVE HALTED...
...COLLAPSED BACK INTO DEATH.
AND THE PORTRAIT IS ALSO BACK TO NORMAL.
IT'S OVER, AT LEAST HERE IN THE MANOR... BUT IT TOOK THE LOSS OF MY PARENTS TO FINISH IT.
YOU DID WHAT YOU HAD TO... AND IT WAS MORE THAN ANYONE ELSE HAS EVER DONE.
BUT NOT WHAT I WANTED TO, COMMISSIONER...

I COULD ONLY BURN THEM... NOT SAVE THEM.
BUT YOU DID SAVE THEM FROM BECOMING PART OF THE EVIL-- AND IN THIS CITY, THAT'S SOMETHING, MAYBE EVEN A MIRACLE.
GOTHAM IS SEALED OFF FROM THE REST OF THE WORLD IN LIFE AND SEALED OFF FROM HEAVEN IN DEATH.
YOU DIE HERE, AND EITHER YOU GO TO HELL OR ON THE RUN FOREVER, BUT TONIGHT YOU FOUND A THIRD OPTION...
YOUR PARENTS MAY NEVER REACH HEAVEN, BUT AT LEAST THEY WON'T BE TURNED DARK... AND THEY WON'T BE HUNTED ALL THE WAY TO HELL.
THANKS TO YOU, THEY WERE BURNED CLEAN.
THAT'S HOLLOW CONSOLATION, COMMISSIONER.
IT'S ALSO BETTER THAN THE ALTERNATIVES--AND AT LEAST A GOOD START.
THE BATTLE'S BEEN JOINED, AND THE STRUGGLE GOES ON.
AS FAR AS THE REST OF IT IS CONCERNED...
WELL, THERE'S ONE OTHER THING YOU'VE ACCOMPLISHED TONIGHT-- YOU'VE EARNED MY TRUST, FULL AND FOREVER.
IF ANYONE CAN CHALLENGE THE DARK LORDS, AND MAYBE EVEN LAY WASTE TO HELL, IT'S YOU... THE BATMAN.
LOOK OUT, BRUCE!
Eh--?
BEHIND YOU!

WHO--?
PRAISE HEAVEN, SIR, YOU'RE ALL RIGHT!
ALFRED!
I'VE FEARED FOR YOUR MORTAL SAFETY THROUGH MY ENTIRE BIZARRE ORDEAL! YOU WOULDN'T BELIEVE WHAT--
AT THIS POINT, ALFRED, I'D BELIEVE ALMOST ANYTHING, EVEN--
CHASH
ANOTHER ATTACK?!
NO--IT'S THE BAT!
MY FATHER'S SIGN--NOW RETURNED!
IT'S HEADING FOR THE GRANDFATHER CLOCK--STILL OPEN!
ENTERING THE CAVE--
"--AND GOING STRAIGHT TO THE VERY SYMBOL IT INSPIRED!"

"DISAPPEARING INTO IT--
"--FILLING IT WITH LIGHT!"

HEAR ME --AND YOU HEAR THE SPIRIT OF THE BAT!
YOUR PARENTS HAVE BEEN SPARED, BUT ONLY BY NONEXISTENCE.
THE REST OF THE SECRET SIX HAVE BEEN DEVOURED.
YOU ARE THE ONLY ONE LEFT. THEIR SOLE LEGACY, AN HAUNTED GOTHAM'S LAST HOPE...

I HAVE FRIENDS...ALLIES.
THEN USE THEM-- BUT NEVER FORGET...

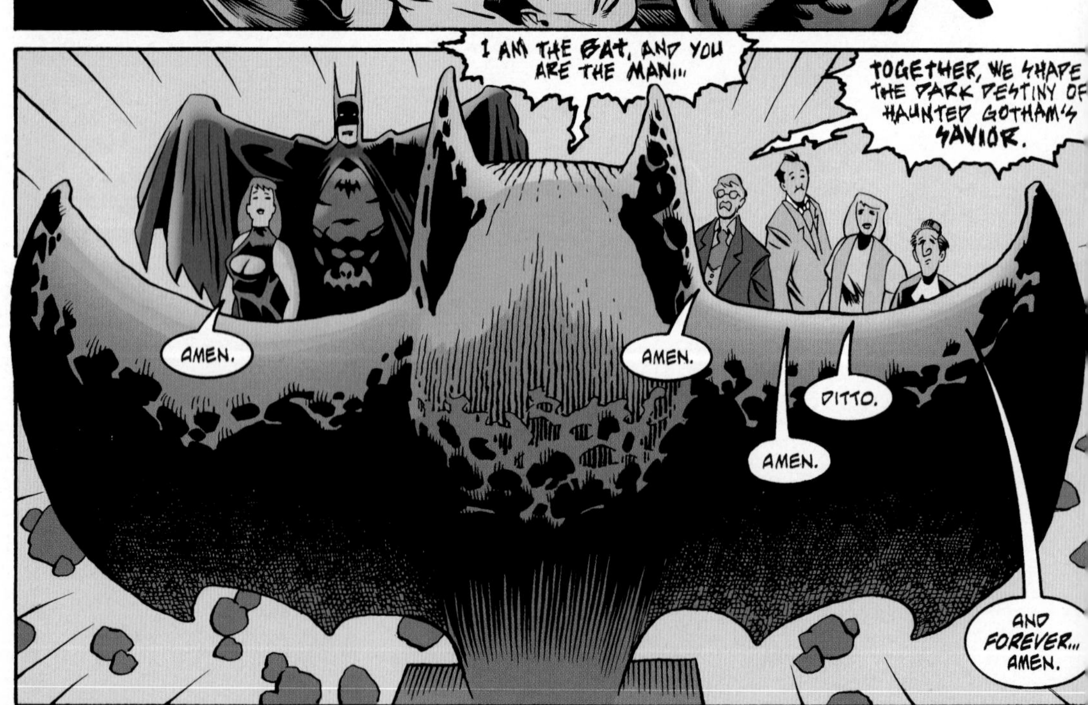
I AM THE BAT, AND YOU ARE THE MAN...
TOGETHER, WE SHAPE THE DARK DESTINY OF HAUNTED GOTHAM'S SAVIOR.
AMEN.
AMEN.
DITTO.
AMEN.
AND FOREVER... AMEN.

FROM THE WRITER OF
300 & SIN CITY

FRANK MILLER

Frank Miller's classic graphic novel features a Gotham City that has sunk into decadence and lawlessness ten years after an aging Batman retired. The Dark Knight returns in a blaze of glory when his city needs him most to end the threat of a brutal new generation of criminals while encountering the Joker, Two-Face and the Man of Steel for the final time.

"Groundbreaking."
– USA TODAY

"It's film noir in cartoon panels."
–VANITY FAIR

BATMAN:
THE DARK KNIGHT
STRIKES AGAIN

BATMAN: YEAR ONE

with
DAVID MAZZUCCHELLI

ALL STAR BATMAN & ROBIN,
THE BOY WONDER VOL. 1

with
JIM LEE

SEARCH THE GRAPHIC NOVELS SECTION OF
DCCOMICS.COM
FOR ART AND INFORMATION ON ALL OF OUR BOOKS!